Uncovering the History
of the
Albuquerque Greek Community
1880-1952

Uncovering the History of the Albuquerque Greek Community
1880-1952

Katherine M. Pomonis

SUNSTONE PRESS
SANTA FE

© 2012 by Katherine M. Pomonis
All Rights Reserved.

No part of this book may be reproduced in any form or by any electronic or mechanical means including information storage and retrieval systems without permission in writing from the publisher, except by a reviewer who may quote brief passages in a review.

Sunstone books may be purchased for educational, business, or sales promotional use. For information please write: Special Markets Department, Sunstone Press, P.O. Box 2321, Santa Fe, New Mexico 87504-2321.

Book and Cover design › Vicki Ahl
Body typeface › Book Antiqua
Printed on acid-free paper
∞

Library of Congress Cataloging-in-Publication Data

Pomonis, Katherine M., 1936-
 Uncovering the history of the Albuquerque Greek community, 1880-1952 / by Katherine M. Pomonis.
   pages cm
 Includes bibliographical references.
 ISBN 978-0-86534-906-3 (softcover : alkaline paper)
 1. Greek Americans--New Mexico--Albuquerque--History--19th century. 2. Greek Americans--New Mexico--Albuquerque--History--20th century. 3. Greek Americans--New Mexico--Albuquerque--Social conditions. 4. Immigrants--New Mexico--Albuquerque--History. 5. Community life--New Mexico--Albuquerque--History. 6. Albuquerque (N.M.)--History. 7. Albuquerque (N.M.)--Ethnic relations. I. Title.
 F804.A3P65 2012
 305.8'93078961--dc23
                          2012033143

WWW.SUNSTONEPRESS.COM
SUNSTONE PRESS / POST OFFICE BOX 2321 / SANTA FE, NM 87504-2321 /USA
(505) 988-4418 / ORDERS ONLY (800) 243-5644 / FAX (505) 988-1025

Dedication

This book is dedicated to the first Greek pioneers who came to New Mexico. May this book be a memorial to their courage and perseverance. They were born into extraordinary hardship, and they met their challenges with determination.

To my father, Anastasios Pomonis, thank you for teaching me a work ethic that has helped me throughout my life, both in school and in the business world. He was a faithful and hard working father, one of the thousands of immigrants who came to the United States in 1910 and worked in the slaughter houses of Kansas City, Missouri; who went back to Greece to fight in the Balkan Wars, and who then returned to the United States to participate in the United States Army with the French Expeditionary Forces during World War One. Upon his return to the United States for the third time he worked on the railroads and mines of the West. And after going back to Greece to find himself a wife, my mother, they eventually settled in Santa Fe where he opened a restaurant, the Mayflower Cafe. Thanks also to my mother, Eleni Vorres Pomonis, for teaching me how to be a *nekokera* (homemaker), and to appreciate my heritage. My love to you both.

Anastasios Pomonis. Passport photograph from 1939.

Eleni Vorres Pomonis. Passport photograph from 1939.

To my son, Yorgos Marinakis, for all your support and knowledge during this interesting phase in my life as a researcher and an author; who suffered through my struggles with me, encouraged me and taught me many research secrets, I give you my deepest love and gratitude.

Contents

Acknowledgments — — 7

Introduction — — 10

1   Independence, Then What? — — 13
2   Crossing the Ocean To America — — 16
3   Finding the Jobs — — 20
4   The West and Albuquerque — — 25
5   Who Was Here, New Mexico Censuses, 1880-1940 — — 28
6   What Were They Doing, Albuquerque City Directories, 1880-1952 — — 32
7   The Greek Immigrants in Search of Health — — 42
8   The Ahepa Sanatorium — — 53
9   Acquiring United States Citizenship — — 74
10   The Women And Their Community — — 76
11   St. George Greek Orthodox Church — — 82
12   The Ledger, the Church's Financial History — — 98
13   The Greek Organizations of St. George Orthodox Church — — 107
14   Greek-Americans and the Wars — — 117
15   The Post-War Generation — — 125
16   Another *Patrida* — — 128

Selected Bibliography — — 131

Appendix — — 133

Acknowledgements

This project could not have been undertaken without the Fellowship granted me by the Office of the New Mexico State Historian. Thank you also goes to Mr. Sarando Kalangis for his financial support.

To all those individuals who have assisted me in various stages of my research and writing, thank you.

> Linda Bahm, Director, University of New Mexico Art Museum, retired and faithful friend
> Susan Calafate Boyle, Historian, National Park Service, Santa Fe
> Michele DeJesus, reader and friend
> Sue Green, friend and Albuquerque's Fairview Cemetery Historian
> Nancy Owen Lewis, PhD, School of Advanced Research for providing information on tuberculosis
> Richard Melzer, Historical Society of New Mexico for believing in my project
> Mo Palmer, reader and friend, Albuquerque historian
> Reverend Father Paul Patitsas for supporting my idea
> Maria Paulson, Secretary for St. George Church, for answering my numerous questions
> Cheryl Raab, volunteer, Albuquerque Genealogy Library
> Jenny Sakellariou, daughter of the first priest of St. George Greek Orthodox Church
> Diane Schaller, President, Historic Albuquerque Incorporated

My research was based on extensive library work at the New Mexico State Archives; University of New Mexico Center for Southwest Research; University of New Mexico Health Sciences Library; University of New Mexico Map and Geographic Information Center, Albuquerque; Special Collections Library; Albuquerque Museum Archives; University of New Mexico Honors Thesis by Rose-Marie Strach; University of New Mexico PhD Dissertation by Judith Boyce DeMark; County of Bernalillo Records Office; Santa Fe City Library; Fray Angelico Chavez History Library; Immigration

History Research Center and the National Hellenic Museum. I am grateful to the personnel of these various archives, libraries and museums. To those of you who allowed me to interview you, thank you. It gave me great pleasure to hear your stories. Thank you also goes to all who answered my questionnaire. Those who produced the St. George Consecration Album, dated November 2, 1952, you did a great job in recording the church's history, thank you. I was able to use some of the photographs and information.

Old lady *(greoula)* gathering greens in the Peloponnese. Photograph by Katherine Pomonis.

Introduction

People often asked me why I was writing this book. As an historian, for me the answer was obvious: because it was a history that needed to be written. There was no history of the Greeks of Albuquerque or the Greeks of New Mexico in any library in the State. Nor was there an archive in St. George Greek Orthodox Church of Albuquerque.

Yet the story of the Greek experience in Albuquerque is unique in the United States. To be sure, we Greeks were part of an economic and social wave that swept across all of the western territories and states. We were part of the western railroad boom that started in the mid-1800s. Like immigrants in Nevada and Colorado in particular, we worked in mines. But Albuquerque was unique in that it was a primary destination in the migration of "lungers" who sought the Cure. Albuquerque, as it so happened, became the site of the American Hellenic Education Progressive Association (AHEPA) Sanatorium, the only sanatorium in the United States dedicated specifically and solely for indigent Greeks.

I also wrote this book because I wanted to know more about my parents' experience as immigrants. There are many questions I wish I had asked my father and mother when they were still alive. This is the closest I could come to that. I cannot imagine what wonderful stories they must have had! I also needed to undertake the task of preserving the roots of this community. If I had not written this story, the future Albuquerque Greek Americans would be unaware of how this community was established.

Last and not least, I wanted the younger generation of Greeks to know the courage of these early immigrants, what they experienced in the way of hardships, and how they persevered as unskilled laborers to become successful in business. Simply hearing the stories of these pioneers can help build one's pride in one's cultural heritage. The Greeks have held onto their identity for millennia. Let us hold onto it for at least one more generation.

As I previously mentioned, mine is the first written history of these early Greeks in New Mexico or Albuquerque. Early on, the Greeks in the state were few in number and could not sustain a church. It was in 1944 that the first Greek Orthodox Church opened in New Mexico, in Albuquerque. I grew up in Santa Fe and my parents would bring my brother and me down to church for communion or special occasions, which enabled me to get to know many of the earlier Greeks here in Albuquerque. I left New Mexico for twenty years and upon my return, I found many of them were no longer with us. Most of the Greeks who are now here had come after World War Two as compared to the ones I knew who had come in the early 1930s. They knew nothing about the history of the earlier Greeks and why they came. They knew nothing about the one and only Greek tuberculosis sanatorium in the United States. They knew nothing about those Greeks who came and eventually established the first Greek community in New Mexico. The history was long overdue. I felt something needed to be done and with the support of Father Paul Patitsas, I sent out 350 questionnaires, received 60 responses and also made audio recordings of interviews of twenty-five of the Greeks in the community. Three have since passed away.

I received a B.A. in History and Anthropology from the University of Rhode Island where I wrote an Honor's Thesis on the rich and famous and how they affected the economy of Rhode Island. I worked at the University of New Mexico's Maxwell Museum of Anthropology, both as a staff member and as guest curator to numerous exhibits including *Greek Byzantium Revisited* and *The Greeks of America*. I served as President of the New Mexico Association of Museums and was on the Board of the Maxwell Museum Association and the Friends of the University of New Mexico Art Museum. After I retired, I was co-founder of the Friends of Coronado State Monument. I am a member of the New Mexico State Historical Society, a member of Historic Albuquerque, and the Albuquerque Archaeological Society and was a CASA Volunteer (Court Appointed Special Advocate for abused children). I am a Santa Fe native of Greek descent.

1
Independence, Then What?

The Ottoman Turks had pillaged and looted Greece for four centuries. In 1821, the Greeks said "enough" and began their war for independence. After seven years of ferocious fighting they succeeded in winning their freedom, but it came with a price; for during those hundreds of years their country had stagnated and much needed to bring it back to normalcy.

Painting of Old Nafplion.

There were innumerable cabinet changes, international entanglements, the frustration of a national aspiration, that is to reunite their "unredeemed brothers" back to Mother Greece (*Megali Idea*, Big Idea), and there was a short supply of resources. By the 1890s, Greece was moving forward economically, but domestic development still needed addressing. Greeks wanted to rebuild their country to its state of former glory by correcting the damage sustained during those four centuries of neglect by the Turks. Optimism in the economy was reflected in the construction of businesses in Athens and Piraeus. Factories were operating at full capacity. Thousands found gainful employment. Enrollments increased in the primary schools, at the University of Athens and at the Athens Polytechnical School.

Construction of public works was moving briskly. A railway connecting Athens with urban centers in the Peloponnese, in central Greece and north in Thessaloniki was constructed. The large swamp in Boetia, a breeding place of the mosquito, was drained; the land in Thessaly was being cultivated; and, most importantly, the Corinth Canal was completed. However, other problems needed correcting. Endemic crimes needed addressing. To name a few, there were the usurers who needed to be stopped from extracting exorbitant rates of interest from poor peasants; the embezzlers of public funds could no longer rely on the protection of powerful friends; and an end needed to be brought to the traditional spoils system for certain categories of civil servants. The armed forces, especially the navy and rural police needed strengthening. All this was costly and being financed by borrowing from foreign sources piling up huge deficits in the budget. This led to more turmoil and instability for the people of Greece. For those living in the rural areas, life had hardly changed. It was still a nation of peasants and of poverty. There was despair amongst the peasants because of a life of unrewarding labor on the soil. These peasants were ignored, heavily taxed, yet they saw none of the improvements that the people of Athens were experiencing. Internal politics had become highly turbulent between the Royalists (the Monarchists) and the Venizelists (the Republicans). It was time they looked elsewhere for opportunities and economic betterment. Some left for Russia, Egypt, or Central Africa; others went to the United States.

Mountain village. Photograph by Katherine Pomonis.

It was in the late nineteenth and early twentieth century that many more Greeks started leaving their country. These were men from Arcadia, Argolidos, Corinthias, Achaea, Elidos, Messinia, Attica, Boetia, Phthiotidos and Phokidos, Aetolia and Akarnanias; the islands of the Cyclades, the eastern Aegean, the Dodecanese, Crete, and the some of the Ionian Islands, Cepahlonia and Zakynthos, and the Ottoman-dominated areas to the east. They were not the educated and wealthy, but the poor. The majority were young males between the ages of 15 and 45, mostly single. They lacked technical skills, but they were ambitious and were willing to work hard. They had a determination to succeed and to better themselves economically.

Map of Greece.

2

Crossing the Ocean To America

The Greeks were the last of the "new" immigrants to come to America during the latter part of the 1800s. These "new" immigrants were the people of the southern and eastern European countries, of which the Greeks were a conspicuous element.

At the onset, these Greek men came to escape economic strangulation. Compatriots already in the United States were sending letters telling them of "golden opportunities." These letters, otherwise known as "chain letters," were circulated widely in the villages. Then, between 1891and 1900, 15,979 more Greeks arrived in the United States. The next group of 167,519 came to the United States between 1900 and 1910. Steamship companies were sending agents to every town in Greece to promote the attractions in the United States. Factories, needing large reservoirs of cheap labor, sent agents to villages in Greece to recruit the labor they so badly needed. Railroad and mining companies were also sending recruiters to bring Greek males to work cheaply for them.

Between 1911 and 1920, 184,201 Greeks immigrated to the United States. This was because Greece was in the midst of fighting two wars (the Balkan Wars and World War One). These young men wanted to avoid the three years service in the Greek army, and for those living in Greek lands still held by the Turks, to avoid serving in the hated Turkish army. The population of Greece had doubled from 2,666,000 to 4,363,000. Its territory increased during this same period from 23,014 to 41,933 square miles due to Balkan Wars treaties. These newly acquired territories included southern Epirus; a large portion of Macedonia, including Thessaloniki; the island of Crete; and most of the Aegean islands.

These immigrants left Greece, boarding ships in Pireaus, Patras or other port cities, to sail across the Mediterranean Sea and the Atlantic Ocean "for an uncertain future, in an unfamiliar place" leaving behind their language, their customs, even their family, to find what? What would the United States offer them? They had heard it was the "Land of Plenty!" They had heard that the streets were paved in gold, and that you could scoop money off the streets and sidewalks!

But first, once in America, the land of golden opportunities, the immigrants needed to be processed through the dreaded Ellis Island, where some feared they would be sent back to their country but where others were allowed to enter...to start a new life.

Between 1900 and 1942, Ellis Island was the United States primary reception depot for immigrants. It is interesting to note that the peak year for Ellis Island was 1907 during which 900,000 immigrants came, mainly from the southern and eastern European countries.

In order to be admitted into the United States, the immigrants needed to be screened. They underwent a physical examination, and a literacy test, and were asked questions regarding their financial status, their social convictions and their past. This screening took place once they entered the main building and checked their belongings at the baggage room. It was during their climb up the stairs to the next area that inspectors visually noted for any problems. Then, they were either allowed to continue or were marked with chalk and directed to an examination room. Here the Public Health Service inspectors, using fingers and buttonhooks, looked for signs of trachoma, a dangerous and contagious eye disease. This and another category known as "a person likely to become a public charge" were cause to have the person removed and sent back to his/her country, at their own expense. The remainder of the newcomers lined up in rows divided by metal rails. Each wore a tag with two numbers printed on it which referred to the page and line on the ship's manifest where their name appeared.

If the immigrants failed to answer the inspector's questions properly, he/she was sent to a special inquiry room where they were either given approval to continue or they were detained. Those that were detained slept in dormitories that separated men from women and children. Meals were provided in the Kitchen and Laundry Buildings where feeding a multitude of different ethnic groups presented a problem. Once they were given approval, they would descend to the Railroad Ticket Office to purchase tickets to their final destination; that is, if they had one. Some were fortunate and had friends or relatives waiting for them. Some had friends or relatives who had sent them a ticket to their final destination. Others had been recruited by labor agents promising jobs.

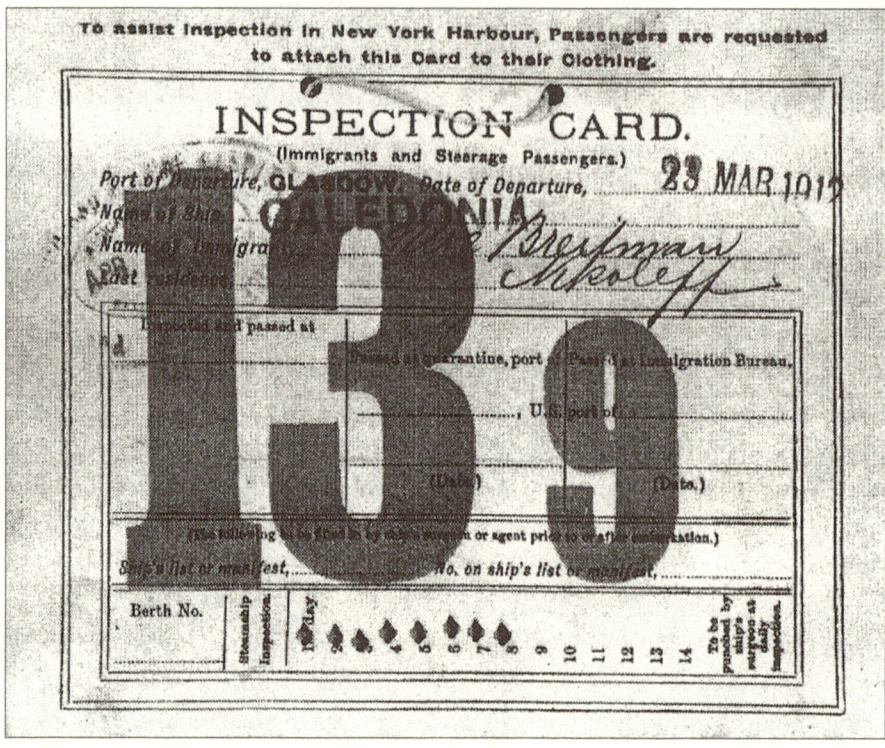

Ellis Island inspection card.

Those who left the island without a destination or a ticket wandered the streets of New York City, lost in the maze, left to survive amongst a people whose language they had never heard. Others fell victim to the practice of the *padrone* system (an indentured labor system that preyed upon the immigrants). This system was outlawed eventually by government regulations.

They came looking to better themselves economically. What they found was a country that was changing drastically from an agrarian society to an industrialized one in need of cheap and unskilled laborers and they were willing to provide that labor!

LIST OR MANIFEST OF ALIEN PASSENGER

required by the regulations of the Secretary of Commerce and Labor of the United States, under Act of Congress approv

S.S. MARTHA WASHINGTON sailing from PATRAS

No. on List	Name in Full (Family Name)	Given Name	Age	Sex	Married or Single	Calling or Occupation	Able to Read/Write	Nationality	Race or People	Last Permanent Residence (Country)	Last Permanent Residence (City or Town)
1	Domouri	Anastassios	20	M	S	Labourer	yes	Greece	Greek	Greece	Iraghali
2	Tripodis	John	19	M	S	Labourer	yes	Greece	Greek	Greece	Lyparissia
3	Andrianopulos	Andreas	19	M	S	Labourer	yes	Greece	Greek	Greece	Filiatra
4	Andronis	Charilaos	25	M	M	Labourer	yes	Greece	Greek	Greece	Faraklata
5	Theofilatos	Theodoros	22	M	S	Labourer		Greece	Greek	Greece	Filiatra
6	Livingopulos	Dionysios	16	M	S	Labourer	yes	Greece	Greek	Greece	Kurgialeki
7	Livingopulos	Harris	15	M	S	Peasant		Greece	Greek	Greece	Kurgialeki
8	Trantis	John	24	M	M	Labourer	yes	Greece	Greek		Constanti
9	Cekes	Georgios	24	M	S	Labourer	yes	Greece	Greek	Greece	Filiatra
10	Couroumalos	Michael	23	M	S	Labourer	yes	Greece	Greek	Checkado	Macherado
11	Chatzaroulas	Eugenia	25	F	S	Servant	no	Greece	Greek	Greece	Argos
12	Bourloussas	Dionysios	22	M	S	Labourer	no	Greece	Greek	Greece	Belousi
13	Coussis	Stylianos	25	M	M	Labourer	yes	Greece	Greek		Caus Jaranga
14	Galamas	John	28	M	M	Labourer	yes	Greece	Greek	Greece	Jalanya
15	Couravis	Athanassios	25	M	M	Labourer	yes	Greece	Greek	Greece	Basta
16	Perifanos	Dimitrios	26	M	M	Labourer	yes	Turkey	Greek	Turkey	Smyrna
17	Csiros	Petros	16	M	S	Scholar	yes	Greece	Greek	Greece	Vitina
18	Cotsovoulos	Dionysios	18	M	S	Labourer	yes	Greece	Greek	Greece	Vitina
19	Carvelas	Constantinos	25	M	M	Labourer	yes	Greece	Greek	Greece	Georgumissa
20	Stavropulos	Michael	18	M	M	Labourer		Greece	Greek	Greece	Georgumissa
21	Capsalis	Panos	20	M	S	Labourer	yes	Greece	Greek	Greece	Vitina
22	Anagnostopulos	Tryphon	24	M	S	Labourer	yes	Greece	Greek	Greece	Vitina
23	Spentzopulos	Lycourgos		M	S	Labourer	yes	Turkey	Greek	Turkey	Smyrna
24	Papoulias	Panos	19	M	S	Labourer	yes	Greece	Greek	Greece	Agali
25	Drivalas	Panagiotis	20	M	S	Labourer	yes	Greece	Greek	Greece	Filiatra
26	Papagiannis	John	24	M	S	Labourer	yes	Greece	Greek	Greece	Filiatra
27	Couvas	Panos	18	M	S	Labourer	yes	Greece	Greek	Greece	Vitina
28	Filis	Athymios	42	M	M	Labourer	no	Greece	Greek	Greece	Agali
29	Zacharopulos	Simos	19	M	S	Labourer	yes	Greece	Greek	Greece	Vitina
30	Catsaounis	Gerassimos	19	M	S	Labourer	no	Greece	Greek	Greece	Santorini

Ship's manifest from my father's first trip to the United States. Courtesy of The Statue of Liberty-Ellis Island Foundation and www.ellisisland.org.

3

Finding the Jobs

The United States was becoming an industrialized nation. The values and lifestyles of the farmers were also changing. They were leaving their farms and moving into the urban areas of the Midwest and the East where they would be able to find work in the factories. The growth of the urban areas was astonishing.

City	Population in 1860	Population in 1900
New York	1,072,000	3,437,000
Chicago	109,000	1,699,000
Philadelphia	847,000	1,294,000

Population Growth of Cities

Industrialization was of great importance to the economic development of the United States. Sweeping developments in technology brought about an explosion in industrial growth and helped form the United States into a modern industrial nation. Factories were opening and untrained workers were able to use the heavy machinery that helped production. The expanding railroad network helped increase trade throughout the United States. It opened the door to the West and linked the Midwest to the Atlantic Coast and connected raw materials, such as coal, timber and oil, to the factories and markets. The United States became a leading global industrial power by building on new technological innovations. By 1900, the United States produced goods valued at $13 billion. Migration, both from within the United States, its farmers, and from the eastern European countries, including Greece, provided the labor base for the expansion of these new industries in the large U.S. cities.

It was into this atmosphere that the young men from the provinces of Greece, its islands and the Greek Ottoman-dominated areas, came looking for work in the United States. They found jobs in the big cities of the Mid-

Atlantic and Great Lake states. They went to New York City, Washington, D.C, Philadelphia, Pittsburgh, Chicago, Canton, and even to Canada as these were the areas men preferred to live as they were able to find employment and receive their wages weekly. They would be near their own people and could enjoy a social life, which they could not have otherwise if they lived in isolated areas.

Many of the immigrants recognized the importance of an education as a tool toward socioeconomic advancement. This way they would move into the middle and upper classes quickly. These newly arrived immigrants attended night schools or public schools. The Greeks prized education. Of all the ethnic groups who came to the United States during this era, it was the Czechs, Japanese, Armenians and the Greeks who devoured education. In their book *Ethnic Americans, A History of Immigrations*, Leonard Dinnerstein and David M.Reimers report that a Chicago teacher claimed "I think I have found the Greeks the brightest and quickest to learn." The Greeks had one of the highest ratios of evening school participants among all other ethnic groups.

Some of the Albuquerque Greeks relate the following stories about how they learned:

Peter (Panos) Karvelas received his American high school diploma at night school in Pittsburgh. He was known as the intellectual of the Albuquerque Greek community. Charles Moskos said that "he was a major influence in my life."

Demetrios (Demo) Pappas tells the story of his father Harry who entered a small college when he was 20 years old in Indiana. With the crash of the stock market, Harry quit college to help his sister whose husband had become ill. He never was able to go back to college, but he was an avid reader throughout his life. Demo felt that his father would have done extremely well in college had he gone back.

George Matsoukas (May) daughter, Georjean Lycas, wrote that her father came to the United States in 1911 from *Lefkohoriou, Fthiotidos*, Greece. He worked as a waiter in Washington, DC, during the day and went to school at night to learn the English language. He came to visit his brother, Tom Mays (when they Americanized their last name, one brother kept an s at the end of his last name and the other did not), in Albuquerque in 1920 and they became proprietors of New Mexico Candy Kitchen. Later in life, May managed the Court Café and the Casanova Cocktail Lounge in Albuquerque.

Peter (*Panagiotes*) Argyres came from Kalamata to Albuquerque and learned English in the evenings at Albuquerque High School. During the interview he recalled working from 7pm to 7am in the Pig Stand Café, "washing dishes and crying the whole time." But he said he learned the restaurant business from the bottom up by another Greek teaching him the cooking techniques. He and his brother owned and operated the well-known café, The Town House on Central Avenue, which is the main thorough fair through (Route 66) Albuquerque. He married Maria *Gregorios* Petropoulos, also from Kalamata who came to the United States and graduated from Newberry Academy. She worked for the Public Library of New York City and then for the Atlantic Bank of New York, a Greek bank.

James Bruskas came to the United States from *Tripolitza* in 1917 and received his education in the Chicago public schools, and eventually became owner of the Hi-hat Nightclub.

Hard work was not a deterrent to these Greeks. They worked as bus boys, dish washers, bootblacks, and worked as confectioners making candy. They worked as petty street peddlers selling flowers, sweets, cigars and fruit from a tray hung around their neck. They worked as laborers in factories and taverns, and in ice cream parlors, grocery stores, and eventually they opened their own business.

William Kirikos came from *Astakos, Roumeli,* around 1910, and started working as a peddler in Wisconsin. He sold newspapers and worked in a lumber mill in Terra Haute, Indiana. Kirikos came to Albuquerque in 1929 and became a well-known business man and proprietor of several businesses — the Coney Island Café, the Pig Stand Café and the Cactus Bar.

Shoe shining (bootblacks) furnished an ideal entry wedge for an immigrant. Angie Pappas tells how her brother came over in 1907 and worked as a shoe shiner until he had saved enough money to bring his brother over. They too worked hard, saved money and brought the third brother over, and then in 1913 they brought their father and oldest sister to the United States. "That is how the family came, little by little to America." Mrs. Pappas (*Angeliki Metrakos*) came to the United States from *Petrina* in 1921.

Anthony Pappas (*Pappadopoulos*) came to the United States in 1920 from Tripoli, Arcadia, to Boston where he worked as a bootblack. He moved to Chicago where he worked for a laundry as their pickup and deliveryman. In 1945, the Pappas family, Angie, Tony and children, came to Albuquerque where Tony eventually opened Tony's BBQ. "He was an inventor and an entrepreneur and a man that picked up fast."

Kostantinos "Deno" Tufares came to the United States in 1908 from Smyrna after having sailed with the Greek Merchant Marines for several years. His daughter Helen Tricoglou states the first job her father held in the United States was painting the Brooklyn Bridge. He learned the restaurant business in Charleston, and moved to Albuquerque in 1936 with his wife Jeannette. She was originally from Alexandria, Egypt. It was in Alexandria that she became an "excellent seamstress and dressmaker at a French school where she learned the art." Deno opened the Cozy Café and eventually the Chili King Café on Central Avenue.

According to Barbara (Vrattos) Vatoseow, her father Elias "Louis" V. Vrattos came from *Stemnitsa* to Canton, Ohio in 1912. He came at the age of 12 in order to work and send money to his mother in Greece, a widow. Her husband had been killed in the Balkan Wars. Vrattos apprenticed with his uncle repairing clocks, and remained in that business until his death. His wife Bessie (Pavlides) came from *Turkomeretis,* an area between Greece and Turkey. In 1940 they came to Albuquerque, along with their daughter Barbara, where he opened the Louis Vrattos Jewelers on Central Avenue. Louis was the first treasurer of St. George Greek Orthodox Church. His Treasurer's ledger contains a wealth of information of the church's first ten years from 1944-1954. See Chapter 12, The Ledger.

Other Greek immigrants found jobs in the textile and shoe factories of New England in the towns of Boston, Lowell, New Bedford and Springfield, in Massachusetts, Manchester in New Hampshire; and Bridgeport and Norwich in Connecticut. They worked mainly as janitors sweeping the factory floors and doing the heavy work in the dye rooms or making shoes.

Anastasia (*Karamanou*) Ipiotis worked in a shoe factory. Her family left *Mekracia,* Turkey, when the Ottoman Turks invaded. They escaped to the island of *Mytiline*. When the Turks invaded *Mytiline,* Anastasia and her family left for the United States going to Lowell, Massachusetts where her brother Steve *(Karamanou)* Karman was living. In 1921, Karman arranged a marriage between Anastasia and James (Piotis) Ipiotis who had come from *Ploumari, Mytiline,* in 1904 to Little Rock, Arkansas. Ipiotis and Karman moved to Albuquerque in 1923 where they opened the Angel Café. They eventually moved to Santa Fe in 1928 "because business was slow (in Albuquerque) and they heard Santa Fe was busier since it was a tourist town and on Highway 66 (aka Route 66)." They opened the Plaza Café, but eventually moved back to Albuquerque. Anastasia died of injuries after being hit by a car on Central Avenue in 1946.

Greeks found a variety of other jobs elsewhere in the United States. The Southeast beckoned a few Greek men, mainly to the state of Florida, where they found work they had previously done in their own country, diving for sponges. They also worked in cafés and many other businesses.

Some Greek men worked in the lumber mills of the Northwest, supplying the nation with siding for houses, telegraph poles, fence posts, firewood and railroad ties. They worked as fishermen or in the vineyards of California.

Farming and raising cattle and herding sheep appealed to very few immigrants because they wanted to make money quickly to send to their families back in Greece. These were the occupations they knew in Greece, however they found them non-profitable and moved on. One of the elders interviewed, Mike Argeanas, tells the story of his father who came from Tripoli, Greece to Trinchera, Colorado, where he farmed and was a rancher and had a herd of 3,000 goats. Because he lost it all in the Depression, the family moved to Trinidad, Colorado, and it was here that his uncle opened a cheese factory and made feta cheese which was shipped to all parts of the United States packed in wooden barrels.

What attracted these Greek men to the West were the mountains and the valleys that so much reminded them of their *patrida* or birth place.

4

The West and Albuquerque

The West was the last area to which the young Greek men came to find work. The Greek Consul General in New York estimated that by 1907 there were between thirty and forty thousand Greek laborers in the West. Posters recruiting unskilled workers as construction crew men on the railroads or in the mines were found throughout the eastern European countries, including Greece. The Immigration Bureau of New Mexico advertised in Europe saying "if you are a hard worker, you will be rewarded." The railroads were in need of cheap and unskilled laborers as were the mines. And it was this work that some of the eastern European immigrants had been recruited to come and do.

The Transcontinental Railroad helped unify this vast country. Opening in 1869, it traveled west from Omaha, Nebraska, through Wyoming, Utah, and Nevada to San Francisco. It wasn't until ten years later, in 1879, that the primary southwest railroad, the Atchison, Topeka and the Santa Fe (AT&SF) Railroad entered northern New Mexico and in 1880 into Albuquerque. The Atlantic and Pacific was another train located in Albuquerque. These trains needed coal to fuel them and the immigrants were mining it in abundance.

Greek men worked on the railroads and in the mines and smelters of the Rocky Mountain region. They constituted the largest ethnic group among such workers, with the greatest concentration being in the states of Colorado, Utah, Wyoming, California, and New Mexico. The coal mines of New Mexico became a Mecca for miners from all over the world with immigrants arriving from Mexico, Italy, China, Poland, Germany, Britain, Austria, Croatia, Finland, Sweden, Montenegro, and, of course, Greece.

Prior to 1880, the mining of gold, copper, coal and silver was insignificant in New Mexico. There was a lack of laborers. The climate was harsh. There was a scarcity of water. There were raids by the Apache and Navajo people. Most importantly, there was a lack of the necessary equipment and supplies needed for deep-mining activity. This would change with the coming of the railroad, whose steam power enabled the transportation of heavy mining equipment for the removal of the mineral wealth lying far beneath the surface. With the coming of the railroad, companies with the requisite capital, machinery and knowhow began moving in. The railroad also facilitated the migration of a needed labor force. The West was no longer isolated from the rest of the nation.

It was long recognized that there were coal deposits in New Mexico, but it was not until the arrival of the railroad into the State in 1879 that mining began extensively in the canyons around Raton (Colfax County) and near Gallup (McKinley County). In their *Historical Atlas of New Mexico*, Warren A. Beck and Ynez D. Haase relate that these mines were producing 90% of the State's total coal output, which in turn supplied most of the coal used by locomotives en route to California. By 1918, 5,000 coal industry workers in New Mexico produced more than 4 million tons of coal per year from 61 mines. It was an explosive industry, in more ways than one.

Dawson, located near Raton, was the largest mining town in New Mexico. Companies were sending recruiters to eastern European countries looking for cheap labor. All that remains of the large town of Dawson is the cemetery where one can find 350 iron crosses of which 69 of those bear Greek names. Their ages ranged from 19 to 50 years old. There were two major explosions, one in 1913 and one in 1923. The majority of these Greeks were killed in the second major mine explosion.

Helen (Kartas) Chirigos remembered coming to Dawson with her father, who was a miner in Walsenberg, Colorado, to the funeral of the men who had died in the 1923 mine explosion. She was only five years old, but came with him and hundreds of other Greek miners to the funeral of those killed in the explosion. She remembered seeing the Greek Orthodox priest going from coffin to coffin, blessing each one.

With the entrance of the railroad into New Mexico, the population exploded as the railroad connected the West to the rest of the Nation, transporting people, machinery and products easily. According to the book *The Far Southwest, 1846-1912, A Territorial History*, the State's population went from 119,000 in 1880 to 195,000 in 1900, and property values jumped in 1880 from $41,000,000 to $321,000,000 in 1890. Two banks existed in 1878 and by 1900 there were 50 that were chartered. New towns emerged in New Mexico including Raton and Springer in the northeast and Las Cruces in the south and Deming and Silver City in the southwest and Gallup in the west. With these new towns, new roads were constructed and new services were needed, such as hotels, cafés and gas stations. The railroad became an integral part of the United States.

Albuquerque became a boomtown, and with it came new services and employment, such as cafés, clothing stores, boot shops, grocery stores, boardinghouses, saloons, mills, hotels, and the first residential development east of the railroad known as the Highland Addition (the area where St. George Orthodox Church is now located). The population in 1890 was 3,785. By 1900, it was 6,235 with more than 20 ethnic groups in residence. Some came to build the railroad and decided to stay. According to the 1900 City Directory, there were 575 men employed by the railroad, along with 60 engineers and 60 fire men, with an annual payroll of $376,000. The rebuilding and enlargement of the AT&SF Shop furnished jobs for 2,000 people. Joshua S. Raynolds, President of the First National Bank, stated that money deposited for the AT&SF Railway Company totaled $500,000. A railroad project from Albuquerque to the San Juan Basin, tapping one of the most mineral-rich sections of the west, was begun. There were five large TB sanatoriums and many hotels with rooms to accommodate those in need. The Alvarado Hotel, operated by the famous Fred Harvey system had doubled its capacity. People were coming to Albuquerque! Buildings and improvements to the value of $4,500,000 put Albuquerque in the front. According to the Albuquerque City Directories, new residential areas were being built having gas and electricity and an abundance of pure water, and the streets were paved and well lighted. What other city in the United States is doing so well?

These early city directories show that other businesses were growing. The second largest industry in Albuquerque was the American Lumber Co., which covered 110 acres and employed 850 men. There was a steady increase in wealth and prosperity and Albuquerque became the chief banking center of New Mexico, having resources of $12 million and deposits of $8 million. The city was also a center for processing of wool, with wool exported throughout the country. By 1910, the population of Albuquerque was 13,000, of which three thousand were here for the Cure—tuberculosis! New Mexico was promoted as "nature's sanatorium for the consumptives" the "wellness country" or the "Heart of the Health Country." Many of the early Greeks came because they had tuberculosis as will later be shown.

5
Who Was Here, New Mexico Censuses: 1880–1940

Official records held in archives of cities are treasure troves of information. The census in particular reveals broad patterns in the movements of the Greeks throughout New Mexico. As noted, they started out in the mines of New Mexico and, eventually, these entrepreneurial men spread out into other occupations, where they realized the Greek dream of becoming their own bosses. Censuses also contain information regarding an individual's origin.

In the 1880 New Mexico Census, no Greeks were found.

The 1890 New Mexico Census was damaged.

In the 1900 New Mexico Census, one person from Greece is listed in Albuquerque. His name was Andrew Nelson, and his occupation was listed as a servant who worked in Albuquerque. Was his name Americanized, or was he the offspring of an English father living in Greece?

The 1910 New Mexico Census lists 165 Greeks (Table 1). There were no Greeks listed in Bernalillo County at this time. However, there were 165 Greeks working the coalmines of Colfax County. The coal in New Mexico was in great demand and the railroads were exploiting this region's rich mineral resource in order to fuel the railroad steam engines. The coal mines around the Raton area—Dawson, Van Houton and Kochler—were abundantly filling this need. The Greek men who were working in the mines had been recruited by agents sent to Greece from Colfax County mines.

County	Town	Occupation	Number of Greeks
Colfax	Dawson	coal mining	114
	Van Houton	coal mining	44
	Kochler	coal mining	7
Socorro	Mogollon	copper mining	1
Grant	Silver City	silver mining	1
Bernalillo	Albuquerque	N/A	0

Table 1

The 1920 New Mexico Census lists 293 Greeks (Table 2). In contrast to the 1910 Census, by 1920 the Greeks entering New Mexico were entering other counties such as Bernalillo. This** icon signifies these men were buried in the old section of Fairview Cemetery in Albuquerque. The spelling of their names is as they appear on the census records. They are:

Daniel Askas; Steve Braketoling, wife Helen; John Depaldos, wife Flora; Philip Doukas; Nicholas Ehartos; George Etefathesiadis; John George; Mike G. George; George Geanno Poulos, wife Mary; **Angelo Glenos; John Goches; George Halulos; Alexander Janos, (sister ?) Angela Janos; James Kliros; **Louis Kliros; Kostantine Koulas, wife Sophia; George Leakan; John Leakan; John Mastoras; Sheer S. Mitchell; Samuel D. Papadakis; John R. Pappas; Beuskaus Pavlantos; Paul Psaltas; James Razatos, wife Mary; James Sides; William Stamos.

County	Town	Occupation	Number of Greeks
Colfax	Dawson	coal mining	55
	Dawson	inmate	1
	Van Houton	coal mining	46
	Kochler	coal mining	9
	Raton	AT&SF, Cafés, etc.	12
	Five other mining towns	coal mining	28
	Gardiner	Patient, TB?	1
McKinley	Seven small mining towns	coal mining, AT&SF	71
Bernalillo	Albuquerque	waiters, proprietors of cafés, bootblacks, proprietor of an ice cream parlor, AT&SF Railroad Supply Department worker, a teamster, manager of hotel, & a baker	30
	Los Barelas	Patient, TB?	1
Santa Fe	Santa Fe	unknown	2
	Madrid	coal mining	1
Grant	Silver City	silver mining	2
	Fort Bayard	TB patients	5
Lincoln	Fort Stanton	TB patients	5
Other	Other	AT&SF, mines, etc.	29

Table 2

The 1930 New Mexico Census lists 235 Greeks (Table 3). They were located in 20 counties with 48 individuals entering Bernalillo County. This** icon signifies these men were buried in the old section of Fairview Cemetery in Albuquerque. The spelling of their names is as they appear on the census records. They are:

George Ades; Nick Augustinos, wife Regina; Tasso Andrades, wife Katherine; Frank Andrews; Daniel Askas; Peter Bruskas; Gus Bruskas; Sam Cardis; Alexander Carrigan; Alexandro A. Caligriates; Nickolas Coloumbus, wife Nora; John Demmis; John Demordes; Sture Dieitaleous; Wm. E. Dolionetes; **Charley Ellis, wife Irene; Angelo Glen; John Goulias; Wm. Janetakos, Lone Karasokyer; Robert Katson; Bill Kerekes; Gus Koulas, wife Sophia; Dan G. Lewis, wife Ethel; Arthur Marinos, wife Rose; John Mastoras; George May; Thomas Mays, wife Marie; Mike Monje; Nick Nacistin, wife Anita; **Peter Nicholas, wife Dorothy B.; Elias N. Nicholson; Spiros Opiotes; James Ipiotis; **Mike Pappas; Toney Pappas, wife Daniela; Louis Poulos; Peter Peterson; T. H. Saaris, wife Alma; George P. Scoledis; John Soter; Dena Spiros (Dimo Spiros?), wife Niki; George E. Thomas, wife Vera; Phillip Vanterice.

County	Town	Occupation	Number of Greeks
Colfax		AT&SF, coal mining	79
McKinley		AT&SF, coal mining	40
Bernalillo	Albuquerque	AT&SF, various	48
Santa Fe	Santa Fe	proprietors of cafés, waiters, bootblacks, proprietor of candy & confectionery parlor, manager of hotel, baker, chef	24
Grant	Fort Bayard	TB patients	3
	Other	various	1
Lincoln	Fort Stanton	TB patients	3
Various, 14	Various	various	38

Table 3

The 1940 New Mexico Census lists 75 Greeks. This number is significantly smaller than previous decades, possibly due to the effects of the Great Depression. This **icon signifies these men were buried in the old section of Fairview Cemetery in Albuquerque. The spelling of their names is as they appear on the census records. They are:

Sam Andrews; Tom G. Angelos, wife Helen and 2 children; George Botulas, wife Ruby; Pete Bruskas, wife Lorene and 3 children; Gus Capels, wife Fannie and 1 son; Nicholas Couloumbis, wife Nora and sister-in-law, Ruby; Charles DeBerry, wife Irene and 3 children; Steve Dikitolia, wife Helen; Charles Ellis, wife Lambrene and 2 children; Anna Hontas and 2 children; James Ipirov; Bob Katson and sisters Alexandra Carrigan and Effie Carrigan; John Kostsikas; Jack Livingston and 1 son; John Lochias, wife Thalia; John A Malanos; Tom Manitaros; Arthur Marinos, wife Rose; George May, wife Jamie and 2 children; James Morris, wife Helen and 1 daughter; Nicholas Nesiotis, wife Anita; Paul Psaltis, wife Christine and 2 children; Theodore Pulingos; Louis Samaras, wife Stella; John George Servas; James Shinos; John G. Sotir, wife Bessie; Gus Theopoulos, wife Mary; George Thomas, wife Vera and 1 child; Stevens Topolitas; **James Trampas; **George Tsintsiras, and **Ernest Vitalis.

It is interesting to note that some of those men and women who appeared in the 1920, 1930 and 1940 Censuses were still in Albuquerque in 1952, as noted in the St. George Greek Orthodox Church's 1952 Consecration Album. Those that appear in the 1920 Census were: George Poulos, Kostantinos Koulas, John Leakan, and Paul Psaltis. Those that appear in the 1930 Census were: Daniel Askos, Peter Bruskas, Gus Bruskas, Steve Dikitolia (Sture Dieitaleous?), Angelo Glen, William Janetakos, Lone (Tom) Karasokyer, Robert Katson, Bill Kerekes (Kirikos), Gus Koulas, Arthur Marinos, George May, Elias (Leo) Nicholson, Spiros Opiotis (Ipiotis), James Ipiotis, and John Soter. Those that appear in the 1940 Census were: Steve Dikitolia, Anna Hontas, Bob Katson, John Malanos, Arthur Marinos, George May, James Morris, Paul Psaltis, Louis Samaras, and John Soter.

The censuses did not record all the Greeks coming to New Mexico and to Albuquerque therefore the Albuquerque City Directories were consulted.

6
What Were They Doing, Albuquerque City Directories, 1880-1952

Greeks may have been trickling into Albuquerque between 1880 and 1910. I say "maybe" because their names might be Greek (See *Appendix* for lists of names of all Greeks in the Albuquerque City Directories from 1880-1952; these directories list residences and occupations.). These men and women worked on the railway, in the lumber industry, and as domestic help. One, Alexander Dim Kassimis of Sidirokastro, was surely Greek. He worked for the Western Union Telegraph Company, and he was the first Greek in Albuquerque to apply for naturalization.

Postcard of downtown Albuquerque in 1911, looking west.

The early Greek men coming to Albuquerque worked on the railroad while others opened cafés, worked as waiters, cooks, chefs, and bus boys and ran short-order lunches. Some came for the "Cure." These intrepid, enterprising men worked as bootblacks, eventually opening their own shoe-shining and shoe-repair businesses and hat-cleaning establishments. They worked as confectioners, opening their own candy shops, ice cream parlors and bakeries. They worked as meat cutters and auto mechanics, managed apartments and hotels, and opened their own real estate companies. Others came as peddlers or salesmen for import and export businesses and eventually opened their own. By virtue of long hours and thrifty living many were able to save a sum of money to purchase their own businesses. After all, they were Greek and they wanted their independence. It was here in Albuquerque that Greek men hoped the years of hardships, both in their mother country and here in America, would prove beneficial. The experiences they had endured had taught them to be resourceful and to persevere. It was here in Albuquerque they were ready to enter the business world, not as an employee but as proprietors.

The businesses of the early Greeks were all located in the very heart of downtown New Albuquerque. Restaurants often changed hands between Greeks, and were often owned by two or three Greeks at one time or run by a family. From 1910–1920, businesses owned and operated by Greeks included the Fruit and Confectionery Co., Albuquerque Café, Mecca Café, City Café, Pullman Café, Liberty Café, Shoe Shining Parlor, Union Shoe Shining and Hat Cleaning Co., Palms Hotel, and Vendome Annex (hotel). Greeks also worked for the AT&SF Railroad, the Santa Fe Railroad, Southern Pacific Shops, American Lumber Co., Western Union Telegraph Co., Parisian Bakery and Ice Cream Parlor, Southwestern Lunch Company, and Jaffa Grocery. They were waiters, bakers, bootblacks, and auto mechanics, and one was a patient in the Albuquerque Tuberculosis Sanatorium.

In his book *The Greeks in the United States*, Theodore Saloutes wrote, "The 1920s witnessed a turning point in the business careers of many." Because of the incessant wars and political upheavals that were occurring in Greece, the Greek immigrants had lost confidence in their mother country. They found that by staying in the United States, there were greater opportunities for them economically. Many of them were moving out of labor jobs and venturing into their own businesses.

From 1920–1930, Greeks owned and operated the Court Café, Mecca Café, New Mexico Candy Kitchen, De Luxe Café, Wholesale Candy Co.,

Joe's Shoe Shining Parlor, Manhattan Café, City Café, Liberty Café #1 and #2, Union Shoe Shining and Hat Cleaning Parlor, Southwestern Lunch Co., 5 and 10¢ Hot Lunch, Alpha Apartments, Albuquerque Candy Shop, the Delmonico Café, Thirty Seven Hundred Café, Savoy Café, Angel Café, Colonia Café, Busy Bee Café, Sunshine Café, Union Hat Works, Duke City Cleaners, Imperial Laundry, Pig'n Calf BBQ, Sweet Shop, Cozy Corner Confectionery, Blue Front Café, Sugar Bowl, Bennie's Barber Shop, Coney Island Café, New Mexico Candy Kitchen, and the Calif. Fruit Co.

10. The Liberty Café, 1919. Photograph courtesy of Mrs. Jenny Pavlantos.

They worked in the services as stockers for grocery stores, waiters, meat cutters, cooks, chefs, restaurant managers, bus boys, confectioners, clerks, a collector, a barber/classical violinist. They were patients in the Jameson Tuberculosis Sanatorium. They even legally incorporated the Hellenic Social Club at 108-1/2 N. 4th Street.

The Liberty Café was one of the few Greek-owned businesses in Albuquerque that advertised in the city directories.

Robert V. P. Katsanis (Katson) was proprietor of the Court Café and according to the Health City Sun (Dec. 17, 1937), the Court Café started neon signs and tiled fronts in Albuquerque.

Postcard of the Court Café.

Postcard of the Pig'n Calf BBQ.

The Great Depression saw the middle class set back abruptly. Businesses were closing, as were banks; there was a nationwide economic crises with several riots occurring in Albuquerque. The Greek immigrants were proud people, hard workers and they persevered and little by little they succeeded—again!

From 1930–1940, Greeks owned and operated the Coney Island Café, Mecca Café, Liberty Café, Savoy Café, Savoy Coffee Shop, Sunshine Café, 5 and 10¢ Lunch, Pig'n Calf Barbecue, Pig Stand Café, Pappas Alex Lunches, Coney Island Café, Court Café, K. C. Waffle House, N.M. Candy Kitchen, and Sweet Shop. The Greeks worked for the Factory and Mill Wood Co. and as a driver for Robert Porter and Sons, and the Coca Cola Bottling Company. They worked as a cook, traveling salesman, steward, waiter, busboy, night manager, domestic, cashier, and factory worker. In 1937 the Albuquerque Greeks founded the AHEPA Silver District Sanatorium for indigent tubercular Greeks.

According to the December 17, 1937 Health City Sun: "The Court Café is one of Albuquerque's bell-weather institutions which for years has acted as the guinea pig for the innovations with which business attempts to make spending money not only painless but pleasant."

Postcard of Robert V. P. Katson's updated Court Café.

Postcard of interior of the then-newly remodeled Court Café, 1937.

Postcard of one of the murals from the Court Café.

The United States entered into World War Two and economic recovery from the Depression began. In his book entitled *Albuquerque*, Marc Simmons states: "The sudden demand of national defense found Albuquerque in a good position to become a major center for military training, wartime industries, and weapons research. One startling effect was a huge influx of government employers, servicemen, and scientists, creating a population explosion and causing a flurry of activity in the housing industry." New businesses were opening requiring labor and services. In 1948, the Atomic Energy Commission negotiated a contract with Western Electric Company to operate the Sandia Laboratory as a private corporation.

From 1940-1950, Greeks owned and operated the Laddie and Lassie Shop, BBQ Restaurant, Town House, Dan & Steve's Barber Shop, Liberty Café, Chili Bowl Café, Sweet Shop, Court Café and Curios, Anderker Cocktail Lounge, Yale Realty Company, Hi Hat Nite Club, U & I Café, Metropolitan Grocery & Market, Carlls Cocktail Lounge, Pantheon Restaurant, John's Café, Blue Spruce Bar, Gus Ellis Real Estate, P. K. Café, Canyon Café and Casa Blanca Bar, Vendome Hotel and Duke City Real Estate Co., California Fruit and Grocery, Coney Island Café, Imperial Café and Real Estate, Menaul Liquor Lounge and Ace Liquor Store, Pig Stand Café, Katson's Drive-In, Blue Room Bar, Dutch Maid Pastry & Deli, Hickory BBQ, Crest-Hi Restaurant, Alex's Café, Union Hat Works and Shining Parlor, S & M Hat and Shine

Parlor, Casanova Bar, Grand Liquor Store, Mazas Fiesta Dress Shop, Doc's Barbershop, Morris Flower Shop, Nob Hill Shoe and Repairs, Imperial Café, Big Chief Café, Serve Yourself Laundry, Cottage Grill, Gus Patterson Clothing Store, Crest-Hi Restaurants, S & W Wholesale Outlet, Doc's Bar, London Hat Works and Shoe Repairing, Pig Parlor Sandwich Shops, Chili King Café, Cozy Café, Atlantis Café, and the Canyon Bar. They worked as automobile drivers, as a salesman for Oestreich-Haggard Agency Real Estate, clerks, cooks, waiters, restaurant night managers, salesman for the Coca Cola Bottling Co., printer for the Gordon Printing and Rubber Co., salesman for New Mexico Leather Co., bar manager, Collections Office of the U.S. Internal Revenue, manager of the Duke City News and Circulation Department, and as a clerk for the Albuquerque Publishing Co.

Postcard of the Pig Stand Café.

William Kirikos was one of the proprietors of the Pig Stand Café. This building still stands on Central Avenue across from the University of New Mexico. The building has had many uses.

Postcard of downtown Albuquerque in the 1940s, looking west.

By 1952, the Greeks in Albuquerque owned 22 restaurants, one radio and appliance company, two cleaning establishments, three barbershops, six real estate companies, a trailer court, a candy making establishment, a children's shop, a dress shop, a shoe repair shop, two cleaners, a men's clothing store, a wholesale outlet, two import grocery stores, a hat and shine parlor, two hotels, some apartments, a jewelers shop, two drive-ins, ten bars; six cocktail lounges, photo service company, a fixture company with restaurant supplies, and a pastry shop. Professionally there was a lawyer and a registered public accountant. In the services were waiters, chefs, cashiers, cooks, bartenders, clerks, sales men, a bank deposit carrier, a mail carrier, a typist and secretary, two painters, and a coffee shop manager on Sandia Base. In 1952, the Consecration of St. George Greek Orthodox Church took place.

They owned and operated the Yale Realty Company, Central Pastry Shop and Café, Royal Café, Dan's Barber Shop, Coney Island Café, P-K , Coney Island Café, Liberty Barber Shop, Town House Cocktail Lounge, Town House Liquor Store, Little Pump Bar, White Lodge Café, Pig Stand Café, Al's Drive-In Café, La Fonda Bar, Canyon Café, Unique Cleaners, Grand Canyon Cocktail Lounge, Shamrock Bar and Liquor Store, Blue Spruce Cocktail Lounge, The Clock Café, Tommy's Place, Johnnie's Grill, Duke City Real Estate Company, Balkan Grocery, Atlas Hat Cleaners, Crest-Hi Restaurant, Cactus Bar, Daytona Trailer Court, Arrow Head Café, Alex's Café, Mike's Café, Pete's Bar, Laskar Photo Service, Bataan Drive-In, Summer's Cleaners, New Mexico Candy Kitchen, Mazas Fiesta Dress Shop, Doc's Bar and Dispensery, Nob Hill Shoe Repair, Nu-Way Café, Golden West Cocktail Lounge, Cottage Grill, Gus Patterson's Clothing Store, S & W Wholesale Outlet, Liberty Café, Albuquerque Import Co., Elm's Hotel and Apartments, Bowery, New Kiva Café, Jewel's Beauty Salon, S & M Hat and Shine Parlor, Chili King Lunch, Depot Café, Louis Vrattos Jewelers, and Billy Zee Restaurant Supplies.

By 1952, there were approximately 87 couples, three widows and seven single men. There were a total of one hundred eighty-four Greeks in Albuquerque—not counting the children. These Greek immigrants had traveled a long way; they had come from the many islands of Greece, from the Peloponnese Peninsula, from the Ottoman occupied lands and from the mainland of Greece. Many of them came as unskilled laborers, had sacrificed and had worked hard but now they were members of the business world of Albuquerque. Later on, the children of this first generation would be embarking on their own journey.

7

The Greek Immigrants In Search of Health

Before the mid-1800s, people were coming to Albuquerque because they had heard it was the "coming town" of New Mexico. According to the Albuquerque City directories, New Mexico was wool-producing country, exporting an annual output of $180,000. The American Lumber Company employed 600 men. It was the center of a vast region devoted to stock raising, ranching and mining companies. The AT&SF Railroad came to New Mexico in 1879 and to Albuquerque in April 1880. It was in Albuquerque's engine houses that major overhauls of locomotives took place and it was the center for supply and freighting. Marc Simmons states in his book *Albuquerque:*

> 52,000 freight cars annually were passing through Albuquerque, and eight passenger trains traveled in and out of the city every day. The Santa Fe Railway's Albuquerque property, containing offices, repair shops, the tie-treating plant, and stockyards, covered several square miles and was valued at 3.5 million dollars.

However, business opportunities were not the only reason Greek men and women were coming to Albuquerque. Many were coming because they were ill. They had been working hard and long hours in the factories and steel mills in the East and on the railroads and in the mines throughout the United States. They had lived frugally and had not eaten well, in order to save money to send to their families in Greece. Moreover, the unregulated workplace environments of the early industrial revolution were not conducive to good health. They lived in cramped quarters while working in the factories breathing in foul air, smoke, and soot. Working on the railroads, men slept in non-vented boxcars where bunks were stacked one on another with mattresses covered with roaches and bedbugs. During the day laborers engaged in menial work with picks and shovels in the searing and agonizing heat of the summer. They cleared land, hacked at trees in the high mountains, hauled earth and rocks, and laid track. They worked in blizzard conditions in the high Rocky Mountains and other times they worked in steady rain for days. For a 10-hour day, they got paid $1.10 a day.

The miners worked in the most dangerous of jobs. They worked day and night, winter and summer hundreds of feet below ground. Some suffered from crippling injuries and some met violent deaths in explosions.

In the cities, manure littered the streets, garbage piled up in front of the buildings and peddlers shared one room and one outhouse.

These Greek men (and women) worked hard and long hours. They were sapped of their energy and were thus easily exposed to a contagious and dreaded disease where the sick were mingling freely with the well. This diseases known as tuberculosis (TB), or consumption or the White Plague, spread with tragic consequences.

Tuberculosis: the disease of the rich, the poor, the black, the white. It was a disease that did not discriminate against the ethnic groups in the United States or anyone else. Here in the United States, the 19th century was called "the century of TB." This disease was highly contagious. It was afflicting the people of the United States into the 20th century and it was the nation's leading cause of death with 80% of the people in the United States infected before the age of 20. Famous people such as Dr. William Lovelace, of Lovelace Clinic, came to New Mexico for the cure as did the famous architect, John Gaw Meem, who designed many famous buildings in Santa Fe as well as at the University of New Mexico.

In the book *Greeks in America*, J.P. Xenides writes that there was a Greek organization in New York City known as the Greek-American Inter-Collegiate League which consisted of leading Greek physicians, lawyers, engineers and literary men who met regularly to discuss scientific topics. One of the topics discussed was the necessity to spread information to the newly arrived Greek immigrants about TB. They did so by circulating to these new arrivals a pamphlet on tuberculosis written in Greek.

Across the nation, New Mexico was promoted as "nature's sanatorium for consumptives," where rest, good food, sunshine and high, dry climate were helpful. Albuquerque became one of the most important health centers of America along with Denver, and Phoenix. Starting as early as 1868, professional journals such as the *Overland Monthly* and the *Out West Magazine* were promoting New Mexico as the "wellness country." The Albuquerque Civic Council promoted the city in booklets and pamphlets as a health resort. These pamphlets were sent to physicians and medical centers throughout the United States. Albuquerque became known as the "Heart of the Well Country."

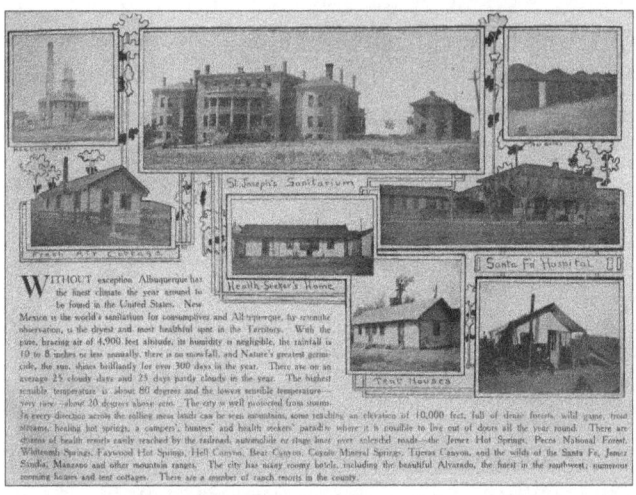

Photographs of Albuquerque's Sanatoriums
from an Albuquerque Civic Council promotional pamphlet.

With the arrival of the many coming for the cure, Albuquerque experienced increasing economic growth. Along with doctors and hospitals, there was a need for banks, hotels, boarding houses, homes, grocery stores, barber shops, theaters and cafés, because many came with their families. In his book *Doctors of Medicine in New Mexico*, Dr. Jake Spidle, Jr., writes that "tuberculosis was one of the central factors in the foundation and development of hospitals across the state; it was the main reason for the migration of hundreds of physicians to the state.... [I]t was one of the basic factors in the peopling and development of the state."

The sick were told to "Go West." Some were cured. Others were not. In 1918 one of the early Greeks who came to Albuquerque for the cure was James Galamos. He had come from Greece, no one knew from where or when. He was 28 years old and had worked in Phoenix as a waiter. He was a resident of Albuquerque "a few days" according to his Certificate and Record of Death. They found his body across the river, in a brush shanty! Was he married? Did his family know what happened to him? He is buried in the old section of Fairview Cemetery.

Death certificate of James Galamos.

Galamos is one of sixty-four Greek men and women buried in the oldest section of Fairview Cemetery on Yale Avenue (there may be others whom we may discover one day). The dates of their deaths range from 1909 to 1941. In this section of the cemetery, which opened in 1881, there is currently no grass, few tombstones remain and some of the graves have collapsed because the individuals were buried without coffins.

Old Fairview Cemetery located on Yale Avenue, circa 2009. The AHEPA section lies to the uppermost left of the photograph, north of the dirt road. Photograph by Yorgos Marinakis.

Old Fairview Cemetery located on Yale Avenue, Christmas 2009.
Photograph by Yorgos Marinakis.

On Christmas of 2009 and 2010, my son Yorgos and I cleaned the AHEPA section at Fairview Cemetery and placed pine boughs and rosemary branches on the presumed (no grave markers) graves. AHEPA is a Greek fraternal organization and presumably a few Greeks buried there belonged to the organization. This organization will be described later in the book.

The author cleaning the AHEPA section of Fairview Cemetery on Christmas 2010, looking east. Photograph by Yorgos Marinakis.

Grave of James Galamos, Christmas 2010. Galamos' death in 1918 pre-dated the AHEPA Sanatorium by 19 years and his grave is located off in a corner alone. Photograph by Yorgos Marinakis.

Fairview Cemetery historian Sue Green was able to find and direct us to the site of James Galamos' grave, on which we placed a small tree. This was probably the first time all sixty-four Greeks were sought out and remembered.

The people listed below are buried in the old section of Fairview Cemetery. They all had originally come from Greece. Unless otherwise noted, they died of TB. Note their ages. They were young! Information provided on each individual came from their obituaries, death certificates and/or other sources. Spelling of their names or home towns are as recorded on their certificates.

Kasta Kakis was a bachelor who owned the California Fruit and Grocery at W. 1728 Central Avenue. He was one of the signatories (Cost Kakis) on the document Authorizing Purchase of the Raynolds' property. He was on the first Board of Directors, and according the St. George Greek Orthodox Church's ledger kept by Louis Vrattos he donated $200 towards the purchase of the Raynolds' property. The house on the property was to be used temporarily as a Greek Orthodox Church. He died in 1955. His pallbearers were some of the well-known Greek business men of that time. For all his efforts he was only given a temporary grave marker. This marker has a cement base with a metal plate attached at the top with his name imprinted on it. This marker was found scattered among other markers. Reason for death is unknown.

Temporary grave marker of "Kasta Kakis" in the AHEPA section of Fairview Cemetery, 2009. Photograph by Katherine Pomonis.

Nick Cardopatis, single, age 34, died in 1934 of TB at St. Joseph's Sanatorium. He came from Scranton, Pennsylvania where he had worked as a carpenter.

Edward Dolopoulas, single, age 28, died in 1920 of TB at Albuquerque Sanatorium. He came from Kansas City, Kansas, where he had worked in various restaurants. No one knew where in Greece he came, or who his parents were.

Nickolas Doukas, age 51, admitted into the AHEPA Sanatorium and was a resident of rural New Mexico. He was a farmer and owned his own farm south of Albuquerque. When AHEPA closed its doors he may have gone back to work on his farm for a while, but had a relapse and was admitted to Nazareth Sanatorium where he died, of TB.

Charles Ellis, a widower, age 57, died in 1916. He worked as a café operator. He died of coronary occlusion.

. Angelo Gianos, single, age 29, died in 1926 of TB at Albuquerque Sanatorium. He came from Dallas, Texas, where he had worked as a waiter.

George Glenos, age 55 died in 1939 at St. Joseph's Hospital and had worked for the Rock Island Railroad as a Section Foreman for 24 years. He died of cardiac failure and possibly TB.

Harry Kanelos, single, age 33, died of TB. He was born in Amalias, and migrated to Chicago where he had worked as a cook. He died in a boardinghouse on Central Avenue, alone.

Demma Nickolas, age 37, died in 1909 at St. Joseph's Sanatorium. She was married and a housewife, born in West Virginia, but lived in Cuba (New Mexico or the island of Cuba?) from 1900 to 1906 and a resident of Albuquerque for fifteen months having come from Silver City, New Mexico. Her father's name was A. Mitchell, a Greek? Was she the wife of a miner?

Anna Nickolas, married, age 20 died in 1925 of TB. She was married to Evangelos Nickolas and was a housewife. She was born in Constantinople, Turkey and contacted TB in Rhode Island three years before. She had lived in Belen for eight months. Her father was Charles Mastaka from Apalos, Greece as was her mother, Helen.

Peter Nicholas, married, age 40, died in 1930 of TB. He was born in Aegena, Greece. His father was Peter Nicholas and mother was Olga Nicholopox, both from Greece. He came from Fort Wayne, Indiana where he worked as a railroad employee in the air-brake department.

Constantine Panagopoulos, single, age 26 died in 1927. He was admitted to the Women's and Children's Hospital for peritonitis.

Mike Pappas, single, age 36, died in 1931 of TB. He appears in the 1930 Census, and was admitted into St. Joseph's Sanatorium. He was a candy maker. His gravesite was donated by one of the Greek businessmen of Albuquerque. He died a pauper.

Nick Poulos, age 47 died in 1919. He was admitted to Presbyterian Sanatorium coming from St. Louis, Missouri. He had been working as a candy maker at the Court Café. He had TB, but died of peritonitis.

No obituaries or death certificates, only burial records, were found for the following men and women. They too are buried at Fairview Cemetery.

G. W. Chearas, TB; Mike Costa; Tom Chugis, age 35, TB; John L. Constantopoulos, age 30, TB; Spiros Contaranis, age 54; Nick Curfodatis, age 34, TB; Peter Dema, TB; Gus Demas, age 34, TB (were they brothers?); John Gavras, age 28, TB; John Geannaris; Sam N. Geannopulos, age 50, TB; Tom Nick George, age 74; S. S. George, age 23, TB; Fotini Guzeus, TB; Wm. Kaps; Wm. E. Kellis, 68; Louis Kliros, TB; Gust Kosmas, age 55; Theodore R. Lellis; John E. Makos, age 43; John Mihelis; George Mitrau, TB; Wm. Niapas, TB; George Papagelis, TB; Mike Sipaka, age 25, TB; Mike Synos, age 30, TB; Peter Tikas; Iannis Tormorus, age 26, TB; John Tregaskis, age 32, TB; Andy Tregaskis, TB, (were they brothers?); Tony Tsaguria, age 28, TB; Katherine Tshamas, age 20, TB; Tony Tsiamas, TB.

These men and women could not afford a headstone. Some were given temporary markers which, as mentioned before, were comprised of a cement block with a metal plate attached bearing their name and sometimes a date. We searched for these grave markers but found none. The Albuquerque AHEPA Order provided funds to purchase a metal detector, which I used to search for the buried metal plates. None were found.

Listed below are other Greeks who names appear in obituaries or death certificates. They died in other Albuquerque TB sanatoriums. Their remains were returned to their home states.

Louis Calogeratos, single, age 18, died of TB, and was a high school student. He was admitted to the Hillcrest Sanatorium in 1933 from Cicero, Illinois. His mother and brother came here with him and, when he died, they took his remains back to Illinois for burial.

Author using the metal detector to search for metal nameplates in the AHEPA section of Fairview Cemetery, 2010. Photograph by Yorgos Marinakis.

Paraskevi G. Giannopoulos, married, age 28, died of TB. She came from Fairfield, Illinois. Her husband opened his own business in Albuquerque while she was in the sanatorium. When she passed away, her brother took her remains back to Fairfield.

George Turles, age 27, died of TB. He came from El Paso, Texas, where he had worked as a candy maker. His body was returned to Omaha, Nebraska.

The Greeks in Albuquerque found stories such as that of Galamos' death unacceptable. They recognized the necessity for the founding of their own sanatorium. In 1936, they purchased the Albuquerque Sanatorium built in 1909. It was to become the only Greek tuberculosis sanatorium in the United States. It was known as the American Hellenic Education Progressive Association (AHEPA) Sanatorium. AHEPA at that time was the leading national Greek-American fraternal organization. The sanatorium buildings were located just northeast of the present Presbyterian Hospital where a parking lot is now located.

Presbyterian Hospital parking lot was formerly the site of the AHEPA Sanatorium. Photograph taken in 2011 looking west. Photograph by Yorgos Marinakis.

8

The Ahepa Sanatorium

ALBUQUERQUE JOURNAL
June 18, 1936

GREEKS BOOST SANATORIUM
Project Seems Assured, Ahepa Chief Says Here

V. I. Chebithe of New York, supreme president of AHEPA, stated in Albuquerque Wednesday night that the supreme council of the order is ready to support to the best of its ability the sanatorium project of the Silver District of the order.

Albuquerque was selected as the sanatorium site at the district convention in Santa Fe this week, at which several Southwestern states were represented. Chebithe said the supreme council will assist in establishing the sanatorium and in supporting members of the order who suffer with tuberculosis and who wish to take treatment there. District Will Aid.

George Ades of Grants, new district governor, who was here with the national president, said that $25,000 will be raised as an initial fund to begin the institution, by the Silver district.

Chebithe said he will recommend a $5000 appropriation by the supreme chapter to start the project.

Chebithe, Peter Tertipes of Denver, Ade, Tony Pavlantos, Robert Katson, Nick John Matsoukas, and others were speakers Wednesday night at a meeting of Albuquerque Greeks and other citizens at the Franciscan hotel, in behalf of the sanatorium project. Local members of the order and those of the entire district are enthusiastic, for the sanatorium project.

The fifteenth annual convention will be held in St. Paul late in August, when the sanatorium project will be brought up.

From this special issue of the *AHEPA Illustrated National Magazine* dated 1937 is an excerpt written by Nick John Matsoukas:

The idea of establishing an AHEPA owned, directed and operated sanatorium originated in the mind of Robert Katson, one of the most progressive and public spirited business men in Albuquerque.

Cover of *AHEPA Magazine*, volume 11, no. 1, January-February 1937.

Robert Katson came to Albuquerque in 1926 and began operating the Court Café. It was not long after he settled in Albuquerque when the need of a sanatorium for the Hellenic people in America was impressed upon him by the comparatively large number of Hellenes drifting into Albuquerque in search of health. Katson appears in the 1937 book on *WHO'S WHO in New Mexico*.

Nick John Matsukas appears in the 1937 *WHO'S WHO in New Mexico*. He was a promoter, entertainment director, a former Chicago newspaperman who came to Albuquerque because he was told that he only had 24 hours to live—he had TB. The AHEPA Sanatorium is the direct result of his efforts. Matsukas traveled all over the United States building up interest and raising money among the Greeks for the AHEPA Sanatorium. Matsukas was quoted as saying that

> TB is the leading killer of all Americans within the draft age and one out of every four young men or woman who died between 15 and 30 died from it. Over 30,000 lungers slipped by the draft doctors in WWI and the cost for Uncle Sam was $10,000 each. You can't walk with full equipment and a have a hole in your lungs.

George Ades (photograph below) first appears in the 1930 New Mexico Census. He was married to an old-line New Mexican family and learned to speak Spanish well. He was the first mayor of Grants, New Mexico. Ades was a tireless worker for the establishment of the AHEPA Sanatorium and the Lieutenant Gov. of the Silver District Order of AHEPA.

George Ades.

The first tuberculosis sanatorium in New Mexico, St. Vincent, opened in 1865 in Santa Fe. Other sanatoriums opened in towns throughout New Mexico—Las Vegas, Las Cruces, Fort. Bayard, Fort. Stanton, Silver City, Chico Springs, Roswell, Watrous, Romero, Alamogordo, Tucumcari, Carlsbad, Laguna, Aztec, Deming, Dulce, Socorro, three in Santa Fe and 17 in Albuquerque. The last one to open in Albuquerque was in 1937, the AHEPA Sanatorium. The buildings of the Albuquerque Sanatorium (see top right picture below) were built in 1909, later used by the Lutheran Church as a sanatorium and then bought to be used as the AHEPA Sanatorium in 1936.

Sanatoriums in Albuquerque from a 1930s pamphlet.

To demonstrate the importance of the AHEPA Sanatorium to both the Greeks of Albuquerque and the Greeks of the rest of the nation, excerpts from newspaper articles describe how the story unfolded. Photograph below is a southern view of the Sanatorium and its bungalows.

July 29, 1936 *Albuquerque Journal*: The Silver District (AHEPA) takes an option on the Albuquerque Sanatorium with the Occidental Life Insurance Co. owner of the Sanatorium. Delegations from the Silver District — New Mexico, Arizona, Colorado, Wyoming, and El Paso, Texas will attend a National convention in St. Paul, August 17 and enlist support for the sanatorium.

July 30, 1936 *El Paso Herald-Post*: AHEPA announced today the filing of incorporation papers with the State Corporation Commission of New Mexico for the sanatorium.

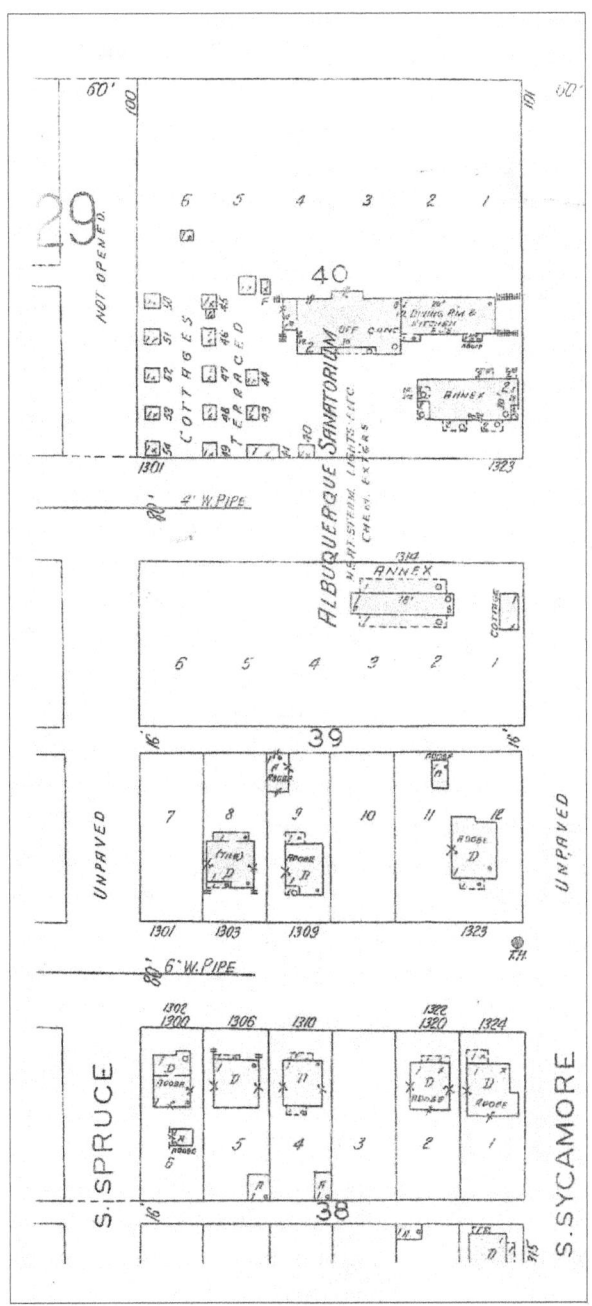

A Sanborn Map of the site of the AHEPA Sanatorium while it was operating as the Albuquerque Sanatorium. Photograph circa 1920s.

Postcard of the future AHEPA Sanatorium while it was operating as the Albuquerque Sanatorium. Date unknown.

August 6, 1936 *Albuquerque Journal*: Albuquerque Greeks set goal for the Silver District to raise $15,000. George Ades names a fund committee: Bob Katson, chair; Gus Bruskas, Tony Pavlantos, Peter Souris and Nick Coulumbis.

September, 1936 *Albuquerque Progress Magazine*: St. Paul meeting on August 23, plans approved for the sanatorium.

October 6, 1936 *Santa Fe New Mexican*: Ades summons Greeks from Santa Fe, Gallup and Albuquerque to meet to finalize national campaign for raising $100,000 for the maintenance and support of the sanatorium and plans for 3,000 attendees at Carlisle Gym dance on October 24, featuring Tommy Tucker orchestra to raise funds.

October 24, 1936 *Albuquerque Journal*: Ad for charity ball.

February, 1937 *Pittsburgh Post-Gazette*: February is the National Dance Month for the AHEPA Sanatorium to help in raising funds.

February, 1937 *New Mexico Magazine*: The Albuquerque Sanatorium was purchased for $50,000 but it was estimated at $250,000. Improvements will be made totaling $15,000. Latest modern scientific equipment to will be used for care and treatment of its patients.

February 5, 1937 Albuquerque's *The Health City Sun*: 50,000 copies of *The AHEPA Illustrated Magazine* will be sent out in several days. Twenty illustrations of the Sanatorium and Albuquerque scenes are included with articles by Katson, Ades, V.I. Chebithes, Supereme President of the AHEPA.

March 1, 1937 *Syracuse Herald*: Proceeds of annual dance for Syracuse Chapter by 500 Greeks will be turned over to be used for the treatment and care of the Greeks at AHEPA Sanatorium.

March 5, 1937 *The Health City Sun:* Dance to be sponsored by Albuquerque AHEPA Chapter No. 174. It will be held on March 6, music supplied by Nato Hernandez and his orchestra (Tommy Tucker's Nationally Famous Orchestra actually supplied the music). One thousand people expected to attend at $1 per couple. Gus Bruskas is the president of the Chapter. Bob Katson, chairs the dance committee. Assisting are: Wm. Janitakos, James Gekas, Odisey Nicholaidis, Charles Ellis, John Gekas, Phillip Voutrin, Nick Columbus, George Giann and Tom Morris.

March 12, 1937 *The Health City Sun*: Mayor Lembke proclaims week beginning Monday, March 22, 1937 as AHEPA Sanatorium Dedication Week. 500 visitors are expected. Opening of Sanatorium will fall simultaneously on the 116th anniversary of Greek Independence from the Turks and the 50th birthday of the Archbishop *Athenagoras*.

March 13, 1937 *Albuquerque Journal*: Nicholas Nicholaidis will be resident business manager of the sanatorium.

March 18, 1937 *Albuquerque Journal:* Dedication banquet will be held at the Masonic Temple on the 24th. Full capacity expected of 500 persons. Toastmaster will be Robert Katson. Greek food will be cooked by ten Greek cooks. Tickets are $3. Events of dedication week include: public inspection of sanatorium on March 24, followed by a sundown liturgy and blessing of the institution. A high pontifical mass will be celebrated by Archbishop *Athenagoras* in the Masonic Lodge followed by Greek Day at the Rotary Club and a street parade; special AHEPA train March 26 to Carlsbad Caverns (this was canceled).

March 19, 1937 Headline for *The Health City Sun* read as follows:

AHEPA SANATORIUM EDITION
THE HEALTH CITY SUN
GREEKS ARE DANCING ALL
OVER UNITED STATES TO
HELP FINANCE AHEPA SAN

March 19, 1937 *The Health City Sun*: Dr. J. G. Harris Physician and Surgeon from Chicago has been selected Medical Director of the AHEPA Silver District Sanatorium. Dr Harris was born in Pylos, Greece, in 1887. He came to the United States in 1906 and returned to Greece where he served in the Greek army during the Balkan Wars in 1913.

March 21, 1937 *Albuquerque Journal*: Guests began to arrive early for dedication. Included are Dr. Minos Joanides, Chicago tuberculosis specialist and chief medical advisor for the sanatorium accompanied by Mrs. Joanides, and Supreme Vice President of the Order, Demetrios G. Michalopoulos also from Chicago.

March 25, 1937 *Albuquerque Journal*: Arrival of Archbishop *Athenagoras*, head of the Greek Church of North and South America. Dedication services will be performed at an outdoor altar beginning at 5:00 pm. A seventeen hundred year old Sun Down Liturgy (*Esperinos*) is to be performed at the (temporary) Greek Orthodox Church. Two thousand people inspected the building, some coming from eastern states and two from Greece.

March 26, 1937 *The Health City Sun*: Impressive ceremonies (*Esperinos*) took place while movie cameras were grinding away and pictures taken.

April, 1937 *Albuquerque Progress*: Nick John Matsoukas was appointed executive secretary in charge of the organization of the Sanatorium.

April 2, 1937 *The Health City Sun*: Seven new patients arrived.

May, 1937 *Albuquerque Progress*: High officials hold meeting to approve expenditures of approximately $35,000 for equipment. The new equipment will be for X-Ray, a laboratory and an operating room. Dr. J. G. Harris is resident superintendent in charge. Staff will be appointed later. Silver District managing board is composed of George Ades, Chairman; Anthony Pavlantos, treasurer and Robert Katson, secretary.

May 29, 1937 *The Health City Sun*: Dr. Harris moves into his home. O. Nicholaides was a former member of a group at the Veteran's Hospital, and is now business manager at the Sanatorium. Chef Peter Zoloumi, comes from Boston. The first female patient arrived, plus eleven more men.

June 9, 1937 *Albuquerque Journal:* Third Annual Silver District Meeting held in Colorado Springs. Nick John Matsoukas gave progress report on the Sanatorium.

October 1, 1937 *The Health City Sun*: New X-Ray and fluoroscope arrived. A new developing room and new operating room were established. Twelve new patients began arriving and a new nurse.

The interior of the AHEPA Sanatorium, 1937.

October 22, 1937 *The Health City Sun*: Total of thirty-three patients representing sixteen states and the District of Columbia plus four new patients.

October 29, 1937: *The Health City Sun*: New directors for AHEPA Sanatorium include Anthony Pavlantos of Albuquerque and James Ipiotis of Santa Fe.

November 18, 1937 *Albuquerque Journal*: Plans are underway to enlarge the sanatorium to increase the capacity of the sanatorium to 125. $30,000 was allotted for immediate use in remodeling and improvements.

November 19, 1937 *The Health City Sun*: Mrs. Christine Hellis Pappas is now assistant to the business manager. The new business manager relieving O. Nicoladis is L. Maniates from Louisville, Kentucky.

November 26, 1937 *The Health City Sun*: Christmas seals are being sold.

NOTE: According to *Wikipedia,* at the beginning of the 1900s tuberculosis was a great feared disease and its harmful effect on children seemed particularly cruel. In response, a Danish postal clerk developed the idea of adding an extra charitable stamp on mailed holiday greetings during Christmas. The money raised would be used to help children sick with TB. Here in the

United State in 1908 it grew to become a national program of the National Association of the Study and Prevention of Tuberculosis. The seals were sold for one cent each that year.

Christmas seal featuring the AHEPA Sanatorium.

Christmas seal featuring the AHEPA Sanatorium.

One seal in the photograph has a date of 1941 and the other may be 1937. They were sold to benefit the Silver District Sanatorium.

December 17, 1937 *The Health City Sun*: A sparkling Christmas tree appears in the dining room. Movies are shown regularly once a week on the new glass screen. Main building and annex entirely full with thirty-six patients. New gas range was purchased.

January 7, 1938 *The Health City Sun*: Patients having fun: Knock Knock—who's there? AHEPA. Ahepa who? AHEPA New Year to you! AHEPA Sanatorium patients give thanks to God for this great institution and its organizers the great Order of AHEPA which is known throughout the world. On Christmas Day Mr. Spiro Kanakis, one of the patients who weighs about 250 pounds, dressed as old Santa helped make the Christmas spirit complete. Christmas carols were sung and gifts were given out. "Santa" said that a great star had guided him through the mountains of New Mexico to Hellenisms' first philanthropic institution, the AHEPA Sanatorium.

Afterwards "Santa" and Superintendent Mr. Maniates trooped though the halls and rooms bringing to the bed patients their gifts. An outstanding gift sent to the patients was donated by three of the regular visitors to the institution. It was a large Mexican basket, more than three feet in diameter and equally as high, piled full of fruit, candy and canned goods. The donors were James Gekas, Nick John Matsoukas and John Gekas. The latter two are former tuberculosis patients, who know what tuberculosis means as they are survivors.

February 11, 1938 *The Health City Sun*: Spiros Shiako (see page 67) and others admitted. Gus Pappas may be going home. (He was Christine Pappas' husband and they made Albuquerque their home.)

February 18, 1938 *The Health City Sun*: Valentines galore rolled in and it sure made the patients feel good. Vasil Ioannow, a sponge diver in his youth, received a large assortment of sponges and seashells. He distributed them among his many friends.

February 25, 1938 *The Health City Sun*: Tom Fillis just got his new choppers and is breaking them in at 15 miles an hour! Mrs. Lillian Nicolaidis is very fortunate as her husband visits her every day. (He had been the business manager of the Sanatorium through Nov. 19, 1937.)

(It is in this column, Feb. 18, 1938, that we find out that it was a woman, around 30 years old, who had taught dancing lessons, who wrote all the above columns for *The Health City Sun*.)

March 4, 1938 *The Health City Sun*: Celebrations are planned by the Daughters of Penelope for March 24-25th. It will be the first anniversary of the Sanatorium and also celebration of Greek Independence Day. A banquet and grand ball are planned. A charge to attend will be $2.50 per plate for adults and $1.25 for children. The Daughters of Penelope and Helen of Troy Chapter No. 19 will present "The *Dance of Zalongo*" play (defined below). Invitations to a score of dignitaries have been extended by the Albuquerque Chapter, the First American Chapter of the AHEPA No. 174 to be their guests of honor. The dignitaries are: New Mexico's Governor Clyde Tingley, Senators Dennis Chavez and Carl Hatch, Representative Jack Dempsey, President James Zimmerman of the University of New Mexico, Albuquerque's Mayor Clyde Oden; AHEPA'S Supreme President V. I. Chebithes and the entire Board of Directors of the AHEPA Silver District Sanatorium and Archbishop *Athenagoras*.

The *Dance of Zalongo* refers to an event in Greek history involving a mass suicide of women from *Souli* and their children during the *Souliote* war of 1803, near the village of Zalongo in Epirus in northern Greece.

Possibly the dinner and celebration of the first anniversary of the AHEPA Silver District Sanatorium. Albuquerque Museum Photo Archives.

March 11, 1938 *The Health City Sun:* Dr. Gekler, nationally known chest specialist, is the new Medical Director of the AHEPA Sanatorium. Dr. J. G. Harris leaves. Gus Pappas finally goes home. He is Christine Pappas' husband. (See February 11, 1938.)

March 18, 1938 *The Health City Sun*: X-rays are flying fast. Anthony Pavlantos is back from a tour of eastern cities in conjunction with the dances. Mrs. Christine Pappas has left, and there is a new secretary. George Ades is always more than welcome to come visit. He is considered a "real man." News: Angelo finally got his radio; Tom Manitaras is playing pinochle but is waiting to hear from New York publishers about his song. Mr. Neciotis, who is also the gardener and landscaper, hears tapping at his window early in the morning. The quietest room in the sanatorium is room five—It is occupied by the youngest patients—Spiros Shaiko, 21 and Spiros Krystallis, 27.

March 25, 1938 *The Health City Sun*: Nick John Matsoukas travels all over the United States for the Sanatorium. Thirty-eight patients are cared for. Louis Maniates, attorney from Louisville, KY, becomes manager. James Ipiotis of Santa Fe continues to be on the Board as does Anthony Pavlantos as treasurer. $15,000 appropriated to repair and refurnish the annex and other buildings giving the Sanatorium a capacity of 92 beds.

March 25, 1938 *The Health City Sun*: Dr. W. A. Gekler, nationally known chest specialist, becomes medical director of the Sanatorium. He is giving talks to the patients on how to care for themselves once they leave the Sanatorium. Occupational Therapy will also start.

April 1, 1938 *The Health City Sun*: First Anniversary gala is described. More than 200 attended the dinner-dance banquet.

April 8, 1938 *The Health City Sun*: Dr. Gekler continues with his talks. Lets patients view germs under the microscope. Contest continues as to who can grow the best mustache. Love is blooming between two of the patients.

June 24, 1938 *The Health City Sun*: Heavy betting is going around on the big fight. They bet the Golden Gate against the Brooklyn Bridge that Schmelling would win. Some bet on horseracing. Seabiscuit always wins.

January 22, 1939 *The Health City Sun*: So much has happened in the last six months, but the author will try in the future to contribute weekly articles. Twenty new patients — men and women have arrived.

January 27, 1939 *The Health City Sun*: Mr. C. A. Alexopoulos comes from Chicago and is the new Superintendent of the AHEPA Sanatorium.

February 3, 1939 *The Health City Sun*: New patients arrive.

Nothing more appears in the newspapers until January, 1940.

January 5, 1940 *Albuquerque Journal*: Constantine Alexopoulos, Superintendent, said Chicago is raising $30,000. At present 50 patients are under his care.

January 10, 1941 *The Health City Sun*: Who is Nick John Matsoukas — his efforts helped with the Sanatorium (His biography appears at the beginning of this chapter.).

August 26, 1941 *Albuquerque Journal*: Over the past four years, the sanatorium has been enlarged, the grounds beautified and land was acquired east of the present buildings. There are plans to accommodate 100 patients which it now houses 40. One main building and a south annex are used. Another building, called the "tower" building will open with the new expansion. The grounds owned by the AHEPA Organization extend from Spruce to Sycamore on East Central and from Central a block and a half south. AHEPA proposes $100,000 drive to extend the facilities. Five thousand national volunteer workers will aid in the drive, describing the institution and the health giving climate and advantages of Albuquerque.

September, 1942 *Albuquerque Journal*: National AHEPA Sanatorium will close due to financial reasons. They will leave all the equipment intact and hope to resume operations after the war. They would offer it to the Government for the duration of the war.

October 28, 1942 *Albuquerque Journal*: The closing of the sanatorium was ordered by the National Greek-American Lodge in Atlanta, GA. on Sept. 1st. Twenty patients remain. Alexopoulos is returning to his home in Chicago.

November 6, 1942 *Albuquerque Journal*: Gus Bruskas, member of the AHEPA Sanatorium board, said that of the 20 patients who were able to leave were sent back to their homes, and the bed-ridden patients were placed in other hospitals and sanatoriums here in Albuquerque. In both cases, the expense was borne by the AHEPA.

Starting in April 2, 1937 until its closing on November 6, 1942, patients came from Pittsburg, PA; Tucson, AZ; Chicago, IL; Kansas City, KA; Denver, CO; San Francisco, CA; Washington, DC; New York City; Martin's Ferry, OH; Coatesville, PA; Warren, O; Waco, TX; Berberton, OH; Omaha, NB; Birmingham, AL; Flint, MI.; Currie, NC; Tarpon Springs, FL; Ambridge, PN; Pullman, IL; Canton, OH; New Orleans, LA; Galveston, TX; Santa Fe, NM; Philadelphia, PA; Troy, NY; Albuquerque, NM; Calexico, CA; Joliet, IL; Rockport, IL; Indianapolis, ID; St. Louis, MO; Utah; Lincoln, NB; Nevada; Seminole, OK; Detroit, MI; and Bronx, NY.; Omaha, NB; Currie, NC; Tarpon Springs, FL; Ambridge, PN; Pullman, IL; Canton, OH; New Orleans, LA; Galveston, TX; Santa Fe, NM; Philadelphia, PA; Troy, NY; Albuquerque, NM; Calexico, CA; Joliet, IL; Rockport, IL.

Those who died in the AHEPA Sanatorium were:

Peter Berles, single, died at age 52, was admitted into the AHEPA Sanatorium in 1939. He came from Grand Island, Nebraska, where he had worked as a laborer on a farm. Buried at Fairview Cemetery.

Bill P. Cardoganis, single, died at age 41. He came from Detroit,

Michigan. He worked as a cook in the café business. Buried at Fairview Cemetery.

Peter Cantos, single, died at age 27. He came from Washington, DC. He worked in cafés. Buried at Fairview Cemetery.

Peter K. Christes, age ?, was admitted into the AHEPA Sanatorium in 1937 and died in 1937. Buried at Fairview Cemetery.

Nick Giameos, single, died at age 35, was admitted into the AHEPA Sanatorium in 1937 and died in 1938. He came from Martin's Ferry, Ohio. He was a factory worker with the steel industry. Buried at Fairview Cemetery.

Jessie Baruchas Hostalis, married, died at age 30, was admitted to the AHEPA Sanatorium in 1939 and died in 1940. She came from the Bronx, New York and was a housewife. Buried at Fairview Cemetery.

Mike Kardiakas, died at age 47, admitted to the AHEPA Sanatorium in 1939. He came from Utah. He had worked as a miner. He died of silicosis. Buried at Fairview Cemetery.

Spiros Krystallis, died at age 27, admitted to the AHEPA Sanatorium in 1937. He came from Ambridge, Pennsylvania. He had worked in the steel industry. His body was returned to Pennsylvania.

Peter Mitchell, married, died at age 53, admitted to the AHEPA Sanatorium in 1937. He came from Kansas City, Mo. He worked as a meat salesman for a wholesale meat industry.

Chris Nichols, single, died at age 30, admitted to the AHEPA Sanatorium circa1939. He came from Chicago, Ill. He worked as a manager for retail grocery.

George Petros, single, died at age 38, admitted to the AHEPA Sanatorium in 1938 and died in 1938. He came from Chicago, Illinois. He worked as a waiter. Buried at Fairview Cemetery.

Spiros L. Shaiko, single, died at age 21, admitted to the AHEPA Sanatorium in 1938 and was a patient there for over a year. He died in 1939. He came from Philadelphia. He was buried at Fairview Cemetery in 1939 with a handful of friends standing by his grave. According to the November 26, 1939, *Albuquerque Journal*, he knew he was dying and had prepared gifts for the medical director and members of the sanatorium staff. On his card to each of them he wrote: "Because I will have business elsewhere on Dec. 25, I am presenting this little gift to you now. May you have a very Merry Christmas and a Happy New Year." The author contacted his sister-in-law in Philadelphia and had a lovely conversation. A few months later, I received a letter from his nephew.

Cement column in foreground is Spiro Shaiko's temporary grave maker.
Photograph by Katherine Pomonis.

Nick Stamos, single, died at age 52. He was a section worker for the railroad. His body was returned to Denver, Colorado.

George Stevens, single, he died at age 35, also known as Kreticos was admitted to the AHEPA Sanatorium in 1937 and died in 1939. He came from Waco, Texas. He was a cook for several restaurants. Buried at Fairview Cemetery.

James Tampras, single, died at age 51, admitted to the AHEPA Sanatorium in 1938 and died in 1940. He came from Oakland, California. He had worked as a cook for several restaurants. Buried at Fairview Cemetery.

John Vitalis admitted to the AHEPA Sanatorium in 1938. He must have been cured and continued to live in Albuquerque. It was in 1952 that he died and many of the well-known Greek businessmen were his pallbearers.

The Greek people of Albuquerque took a great deal of interest in helping and entertaining the patients at the Sanatorium. Mary (Ipiotis) Shields was the daughter of James and Anastasia Ipiotis who came to Albuquerque around 1923. Mary remembers her mother baking Greek butter cookies (*kourambiathes*) and nut and honey dessert (*baklava*) to take to the patients at AHEPA Sanatorium. Her mother had a lot of sympathy for those people as she was a survivor because her husband once had TB, the reason they had moved to Albuquerque.

Some of the Greeks of this particular time frame who had come to Albuquerque due to respiratory problems such as tuberculosis or asthma and others who had arthritis problems contributed greatly to the community. Among the best known were: Dorothy Kapnison, Demo Pappas, Dean Pappas, William Assimakis, John Benakis, George J. Giann, James Ipiotis, William Janetakos, Constantine Liakoupoulos, Nick John Matsoukas, George Mavromatis, and sister Helen Mavromatis, Gus Pappas, Diamond Peterson, Bessie Vrattos, Stella Zavakos, Basil Laskurakis, Theodore Tufares, John Chirigos, and Potitsa Argos.

The announcement below comes from the *1942 Tuberculosis Sanatorium Directory* published by the National Tuberculosis Association:

> Ahepa National Sanatorium, 1301 Gold Avenue (1937): A non-profit institution. Patients are restricted to Greeks and members of the immediate family. Admits all stages of tuberculosis in any form. Capacity: 46. Rates: Free; indigents only. Diagnostic and treatment facilities: Surgical procedures are available through local specialists and surgeons. Resident Staff: nursing: 4, including 1 graduate registered nurse: X-ray and laboratory technicians. Out-patient service available, rx refills. Medical director: Dr. W. A. Gekler. Apply to C. A. Alexopoulos, Superintendent.

What Happened after the 1942 closing of the Property?

The property was placed on the market for sale soon after it ceased to be a sanatorium. Contracts for sale to two different sets of purchasers were signed. Both deals fell through.

April 30, *1943 Santa Fe New Mexican*: According to Dr. James R. Scott, State Health Director, the AHEPA Sanatorium building is under consideration for venereal disease hospital.

May 1, 1943 *Santa Fe New Mexican*: Use of buildings hinges on a federal allotment.

August 31, 1944 *Santa Fe New Mexican*: Bids to open at State Purchasing Agent for alterations and repairs to buildings of the New Mexico Intensive Treatment Center (NMITC)

September 13, 1944 *Santa Fe New Mexican*: Sixty-seven patients admitted to the NMITC for treatment of gonorrhea and syphilis.

October 6, 1944 *Las Vegas Daily Optic:* Fifty-one more patients were sent to the NMITC.

Shown on the 1948 Sanborn Map were these words: New Mexico Intensive Treatment Center (NMITC) operated by the State and leased from AHEPA National Sanatorium (owners).

June 8, 1951 *Albuquerque Tribune*: NMITC will close June 30.

July 14, 1951 *Albuquerque Tribune*: There is a possibility of leasing the old AHEPA Sanatorium located at 1303 E. Gold, to a group of doctors for a clinic This idea is being studied by the Order of AHEPA.

July 20, 1951 *Albuquerque Tribune*: The AHEPA Sanatorium property is ready to be leased according to Gus Bruskas, newly elected board member of the sanatorium committee. He attended an AHEPA district convention in Denver as a delegate this week. The AHEPA has granted him authority to proceed with leasing and repairing of the property.

October 16, 1951 *Albuquerque Journal*: The Supreme Lodge of the Order of AHEPA, currently in session in Albuquerque will decide today what to do about the old AHEPA Sanatorium. A series of meetings, which began Sunday at the Hilton hotel, will continue until Wednesday. The sanatorium figured in a District Court suit filed against National Order of AHEPA and the AHEPA Silver District Sanatorium, Inc. was settled on Monday. A $100,000 damage suit brought by Berger, Briggs and Hicks, a real estate firm, was settled out of court for $17,000. Peter N. Chumbris, a Greek lawyer and local adviser to the Sanatorium Board, said the Supreme Lodge met here in one of a series of regional conferences around the nation. The Albuquerque meeting was called to decide what to do with the sanatorium.

October 16, 1951 *Albuquerque Tribune*: Tentative plans for the erection at the site of the sanatorium for a million dollar office building for physicians were discussed. The Order of AHEPA has decided to use the valuable site as an income producing property with profits going to charitable institutions at less valuable locations.

October 17, 1951 *Albuquerque Journal*: AHEPA to retain old sanatorium and offer it for rent. Preliminary plans are to raise a million-dollar structure. The present building might be remodeled and used as a hotel.

April 18, 1952 *Albuquerque Journal*: Albuquerque's Army and Air Force recruiting station will move to new quarters by May 20. The new quarters will be in the AHEPA Building.

April 24, 1961 *Albuquerque Tribune:* Fire destroys roof of an empty building. Apparently the fire started in the attic of the long structure that resembles a set of duplex apartments. Building was part of the property belonging to the Greek Order of AHEPA and is across the street from the main structure. The entire structure was badly damaged. (This may have been when this building was torn down.)

April 28, 1961 *Albuquerque Tribune*: Mr. Bruskas of Yale Realty Co. said the building had formerly housed six apartments.

Newspaper advertisement for Yale Realty.

August 3, 1962 *Albuquerque Tribune:* Gus D. Bruskas, agent for The Order of AHEPA requests change of zone from R-J (residential) to O-I (office) for Lots 7 through 12, Block 40. This is the entire property on which the main buildings, the annex and the many cottages stood. (Were the buildings torn down by this time?).

May 7, 1971 *Albuquerque Tribune*: The Order of AHEPA announced today it is seeking to sell or lease its nearly three acres of property in the southeast area of Albuquerque. This **vacant** land is located south of Central Avenue, between Gold, Sycamore and Spruce, S.E. plus a quarter of the block across Gold at Sycamore, S.E.

Steve Betzelos, Supreme Governor of the Order of AHEPA announced today that "It is the only remaining large piece of vacant land near the downtown area in the southeast part of the city." The Albuquerque chapter, at that time, was headed by Tom Manolis.

In 1971, Presbyterian Hospital bought the land for $195,000 and turned it into a parking lot (See Figure 27, above).

A Greek Tragedy?

In addition to the tragedies of the illnesses and deaths of the sanatorium's patients, there was another Greek tragedy associated with the sanatorium: litigation over the sale of the sanatorium threatened to tear apart the Albuquerque Greek community. In October 1945, George Ades offered to buy the sanatorium from the (National) Order of AHEPA for $50,000. He stated that he had a partner but did not state his partner's name. As it turned out, his partner was Gus Bruskas. The Order of AHEPA initially agreed to the sale, but then apparently other Greeks in Albuquerque alleged that Ades and Bruskas were misrepresenting the value and that it was actually worth much more. The Order subsequently revoked their agreement to sell to Ades and Bruskas. Ades and Bruskas in turn alleged fraud against the Order and sued to enforce the agreement. The attorneys for the Order raised a defense under the Statute of Frauds (because the names of both buyers had not been adequately disclosed in the written offer) and won both at trial and appeal in the New Mexico Supreme Court (May 22, 1947). In December 1945 while the case was at trial, the Order offered the sanatorium for sale. Berger and Briggs real estate company made an offer. When the Order did not accept the offer, Berger and Briggs sued (August 27, 1947). That case was settled at trial with an award to Berger and Briggs for $17,500 (October 15, 1951). Attorney O'Sullivan, who represented the Silver District (Albuquerque) AHEPA in the Berger and Briggs case, then sued the Silver District AHEPA $10,000 for additional attorney's fees. He also alleged that the Silver District AHEPA, which was then attempting to transfer title of the sanatorium to the Order of AHEPA, was doing so in order to divest themselves of their assets so they would not have to pay O'Sullivan. The Silver District AHEPA contributed $5,000 for the sanatorium, while the Order of AHEPA and other Districts contributed the rest of the $50,000 purchase price, yet title to the property remained in the name of the Silver District. We do not know the outcome of this last case.

It is unclear whether time justified Ades' offer. Remember that Ades offer to buy the property in 1945 for $50,000, and that Presbyterian bought the property in 1971 for $195,000. According to the Minneapolis Federal Reserve calculator, $50,000 in 1945 dollars is only $112,507 in 1971 dollars, which falls short of the actual $195,000 sales price by 42.3%. To make $195,000 in 1971 dollars, you would need $86,700 in 1945 dollars, or $36,700 more than Ades' $50,000. However, the $50,000 does not include the additional cost of litigation and settlement, which was at least $27,500, a number very close to the $36,700.

9

Acquiring United States Citizenship

Naturalization means citizenship is granted to a non-citizen. Becoming a Naturalized Citizen was a complicated path involving:

> Lawful entry into the United States through a port of entry.
> Completion of a Certificate of Arrival.
> Declaration of Intention after two years of residency.
> A Deposition of Witnesses would be taken of persons who had known applicant for the previous five years.
> Exclusion or formal denial due to claims of exemption for military service during World War I and World War II. (In other words, if drafted, and they claimed to be exempt because they would not give up Greek allegiance, they were denied citizenship.)
> Oath of Allegiance was taken where the applicant gave up foreign allegiance, promising to obey the United States Constitution and its laws.

Below is a partial list of Greek men and women in Albuquerque who petitioned for Naturalization and were either accepted or denied.

Alexander Dim Kassimis was the first Greek to Petition for Naturalization in Albuquerque. He came to the United States in 1905 from Sidirokastro and to Albuquerque in 1911. He worked for Western Union Telegraph Company as a telegraph operator. The other Greek men who appllied for Naturlization were: George K. Argyres, Steven Nicholas Belilis, Christ Bress, Gus Brouskas, Steve (Stauros) Dikitolia, Carrey G. George (Cariakos Georgia Georgakis), Steve Karman (Styleaneous Karmanos or Karamanou), Peter (Panos) Karvelas, Costandino Koulas, George Mavromatis, George H. May (Matsosukas), Charles (Photios) Moskos, Anthony Pavlantos, Peter Rallils, Kostantinos Tufares, and Louis (Elias) V. Vrattos.

The women who applied for Naturalization were: Katherine Bruskas, Georgia Chalamidas, Lela Chalamidas, Irene Collaros, Ourania Kazanas and Jeanette Tufares.

The fact that they applied for Naturalization demonstrates their intent to assimilate into American culture. In general, the Greeks in the United States were slow to become naturalized citizens. To many it meant renouncing their heritage, hence their identity. So why did these immigrants in Albuquerque scramble to become American citizens? These "pioneer" Greeks had left their country to better themselves economically, had worked hard and now many had established themselves in their own businesses. Perhaps they now realized that they wanted to make the United States their permanent homes. Greece no longer could provide work opportunities; the United States could. In addition, the U.S. was restricting immigration. These individuals must have felt pressure to take advantage of the good fortune of their positions in the New World. In 1921, 28,000 Greeks entered the United States, but with the passage of restrictive immigration laws culminating with the Reed-Johnson Act of 1924, only 100 Greeks were allowed to enter the United States each year. This number was increased, in 1929, to 307 per year and remained so for the next three decades.

10

The Women and the Community

By the 1920s the Greek men were becoming prosperous. They were owners of small businesses. They were moving into the middle class and were now beginning to think about marriage. Since there was a scarcity of Greek women, some men married non-Greeks. But others preferred a woman of their own nationality and religion. Some of these men journeyed to Greece in search of a wife. Others had prospective brides sent to them, whose friend or relative in Greece had vouched for. Some had friends living in other parts of the United States who had sisters of marriageable age and agreements of marriage were made. There were also picture-order brides or bridegrooms.

Anthony Pavlantos, in 1917, was a partner with two cousins, Bill and Paul Psaltis, in the Liberty Café. Mrs. Provas, an elderly Greek woman, told him of a nice young lady in Chicago that would make him a good wife. He and Bessie were married in 1918.

Victoria Poulos Moskos tells how her grandparents Paul (Simos) Symon and Mary (Moros) married. Paul had migrated to Alaska in the late 1800s with two other Greek young men. One had a sister (Mary) and the marriage would be arranged.

Paul (Simos) Symon and Mary (Moros) Symon.

Angie (Angeliki) Pappas tells how she and Tony met. He had been dating a German girl and they were going to get married. An old man told him he needed to marry a Greek woman. He broke if off with her and told everyone he was looking to find a nice Greek girl. Angie had a cousin in Chicago where Tony lived and he told him "I have a cousin in Dayton, Ohio." Well, Tony said, "bring her here." They met on August 15 and were married on September 30th. "Our life was a very, very happy life." Tony passed away at the age of 93 and Angie at 99.

Demo Pappas said that a *proxinia* (match making) brought his parents together. His mother happened to be from the same area in Greece, *Gargayannie*, as his father. The families said, "We know your family, you know our family, we are all good people." That is how they did it then and they got married.

Niki Daskalos came to the United States as a young girl with her two brothers and lived in Las Vegas, New Mexico with their uncle. Niki decided that she wanted to marry a Greek and remembered a man in her village. She wrote to her mother, pictures were exchanged and the marriage was arranged. Tom Manole came from Greece to marry Niki.

Peter (Panagiotes) Argyres, owner of the Town House Restaurant on Central Avenue, wanted to go back to Greece to find a wife. A friend in Greece wrote him "Why come here to Greece when there is a lovely Greek girl in New York City." He called Maria Petropoulos and told her he would like to send her the fare to come to Albuquerque so they could meet each other and, "if I like you and you like me, we can get married." They were married within three days. He said, "There isn't a couple that don't have their differences, but I read that when you go to bed and turn the light out, it is a new day for you. Don't hold a grudge."

James Frangos was on an AHEPAN excursion to Greece in 1947 when a friend pointed out Bessie to him. They were married within the week.

Louis Karvelas tells how, after his father (Panos or Peter) had fought in World War One and, after working for a while, decided he wanted to get married. Friends gave him the names of eligible young "damsels" in Greece and in 1925 he went in search of one of these young damsels. Her name was Angelica.

A very special story is about Christopher Evangel and his wife Effie. They had met years before in Canada and fell in love. Christopher went off to war and they lost contact with one another. When Christopher came back from the war he married a woman in Santa Fe. Their marriage did not last and he moved to Albuquerque where he and Effie met again—and were married.

The patterns in the changing addresses of the Greek men in the Albuquerque City directories show that they were moving away from boardinghouses and hotels along Central Avenue or areas near the railroad tracks and purchasing houses for their new wives in the Huning Highland District. This district was located just east of the railroad and was the first suburb of Albuquerque. Property ownership was an indication of economic success. They began emerging as a Greek-American bourgeoisie.

It was with the arrival of Greek wives that the *kinotis* or community was anchored here in Albuquerque. These young women, at least initially, could not speak English and thus was formed an intimate circle of Greek women with whom they also shared other unifying factors: their heritage and religion.

Gathering of Greek women and children, circa mid-to late-1930s.
Photograph courtesy of Estate of Helen Pomonis.

The few people who remember the early days speak fondly of how close the families were. "We were like one big family." It was not a large community and everyone knew each other. The women and their children would go together to Roosevelt Park, where they would have a picnic, the children would play together and the women would sew and exchange memories and ideas When there was a Saint Day gathering or baptism everybody was invited. It was the women who brought everyone together to celebrate these special occasions. If there were two or more celebrating their Saint Day, they would coordinate—"You have it at your house in the afternoon and I will have it at my house in the evening."

On Mother's Day the older Greek women were honored by the women of the community. A tea was given them and the daughters would dress up in their finest to show how very much they appreciated what the elders had done to develop their *kinotis*.

Mother's Day honoring the elder Greek mothers.

Amazetta Mays, daughter of George Mays, recalls making *fillo* (paper-thin sheets of unleavened flour dough used to make *baklava*) and using the dining room table to spread out the dough on floured sheets. She recalls the holidays were always celebrated and the women always cleaning and cooking and visiting. She particularly loved Easter because the men would go up into the mountains, dig a pit, and roast either a whole lamb or pig. Then the women would follow with many other dishes. After eating and drinking, the men would get up and dance. Dance still plays a very important role in the Greek life as it brings the community together and it expresses the dancer's inner feelings.

Picnic in the mountains. Photograph courtesy of Estate of Helen Pomonis.

Picnic in the mountains. Left to right: Niki Daskalos, Harry Dakos, Gus Daskalos, Pete and Chris Daskalos

May also said something that I had not heard for many years—she remembers watching a Greek woman placing *vendoozes* on another person! It is an old, country method of ridding someone of chest colds.

"The Greeks took care of each other and brought food to the sick in their homes." She said they were a tight-knit group. "If someone was sad because they missed their family in Greece one of the women would come and talk with them and bring them soup."

The bachelors were always welcomed to a home for dinner and holidays. They came in their overcoats that were long, almost to their ankles. When they heard a Greek was opening up a business they would go and patronize the new store or restaurant. If the owner refused to take money, they would argue with him but always ended up leaving their money on the table. And when the children went into the new establishment they would always get a treat...an ice cream cone, a hot dog, candy, money or even a free shoe shine!

It was when the wives came to Albuquerque that the Greek *kniotis* was established. These women were the socializing agents. They brought everyone together, whether they were married or not. Prior to the women coming to the United States, the men would congregate in coffee houses or meeting rooms and play cards and argue vociferously about politics. Now the men were coming together with their wives and children, as a cohesive group of families with a shared identity. These men and women spoke the same language, cooked the same type of food, shared their cultural history and heritage and most importantly, shared their spirituality. They all lived close to each other, in the same area, the Huning Highland. There was a sense of belonging. This commonality helped enhance the overall health of the community.

It was the married women who made the Hellenic Community of Albuquerque happen. They wanted to retain their heritage for the children they had or would eventually have. From the old country, they brought a piece of their *patrida* or birth place to Albuquerque. They brought with them their family traditions and their religious beliefs. These all provided them with a feeling of security.

There was only one thing missing for them: there was no church.

11
St. George Greek Orthodox Church

Here in the United States, Greek Orthodox churches originated from the desires and the actions of the Greek immigrants—in the case of Albuquerque, mainly the actions of the Hellenic Community or the *kinotis*. The Greek Orthodox Church had kept alive the Greek ideal of nationalism during the many centuries of Ottoman Turk occupation. The Greek immigrants themselves also felt nationalism for their mother country, even though they had moved to the United States. For this reason, some had refused to register to fight for the United States in the First World War. This later came back to haunt them when they applied for naturalization. Others registered and earned their U.S. citizenship. In all cases, however, they did not abandon their Greek identity, which was most expressed through their Orthodox religion.

The early Greeks in Albuquerque would bring in itinerant priests from Pueblo, Colorado to perform marriages, funerals and baptisms which were performed in galvanized tubs. Helen (Tufares) Tricoglou and Christine (Tufares) Argeanas remember these visiting priests would perform services in the cabins that were part of the AHEPA Sanatorium.

In fact, the first Greek Orthodox Church in Albuquerque and in New Mexico may have been the St. Barbara Hellenic Orthodox Church at the AHEPA Sanatorium. An article on page 3 of the March 11, 1937, *Albuquerque Journal* states as follows:

GREEK ORTHODOX CHURCH HERE TO BE FIRST IN THE STATE

Establishment of the first Greek Orthodox Church in New Mexico as part of the AHEPA Silver District Sanatorium was announced Wednesday after George Ades, district governor of the AHEPA organization, had applied for an ecclesiastical charter from the Greek Archdiocese of North and South America through Archbishop *Athenagoras*.
Granting of the charter is a simple routine. New Mexico is the last State in the union to have a Greek Orthodox Church.

The ecclesiastical jurisdiction of the permanent priest, who will reside at the AHEPA Sanatorium, will extend over all New Mexico and he will not only officiate here, but also in Gallup, Santa Fe and other New Mexico points.

Selection of the pastor will be made by Archbishop *Athenagoras*, but contrary to the practice among Greek churches in this country he will be under the jurisdiction of the sanatorium.

At 10:30 A.M., church services at St. Barbara Hellenic Orthodox Church on the sanatorium grounds will be held, conducted by the Rev. *Polichronis* of Pueblo, Colorado.

This church, if it was a church, apparently closed when the AHEPA Sanatorium closed. One could say, the history of St. George Greek Orthodox Church began in 1907 when J. M. Raynolds, President of the First National Bank of Albuquerque, had a house built in the Huning Highland Neighborhood on the 300 block of High Street. The exterior walls of the house and the wall surrounding the property were built with "cast stone" material. This "cast stone" was a cement block faced on the exterior side to look like stone and manufactured by Angelo DeTuillio. His factory and residence stood on Copper between Edith and Arno. DeTuillio was trained as an architect and an engineer in Italy. All that remains of this stone work on the church property is the wall surrounding the property, which has been stuccoed over.

On December 23, 1936, the Raynolds were having the interior of their house painted as they were entertaining on Christmas Day. Mrs. Raynolds had asked Mr. Gay, the painter, to paint a closet and he told her that she needed to pay him first. She told him to go home because he was drunk. They argued and he left but returned later and continued to argue with her. Mr. Raynolds came into the kitchen and told him to come into the living room so they could discuss the situation. When they entered the living room, Mr. Gay said he had something for them, pulled out a .38-caliber pistol and shot Mrs. Raynolds in the stomach. Mr. Raynolds grappled with Mr. Gay and the Raynolds daughter ran out of the room, returning with a gun. Mrs. Raynolds, who was still on her feet, grabbed the gun and shot Mr. Gay in the head. She then collapsed. She died that evening and he, the next day.

Front page of *Albuquerque Journal*, December 23, 1936.

The Raynolds House

The house stood vacant for a number of years after the shooting and in 1944 Mr. Raynolds went to Gust Ellis, a Greek real estate agent, and asked him to try and sell the house. Gust tried for several months. The price was very good and he talked to several Greeks about purchasing it. As was stated in the previous chapter, the time had come for the Greek community to establish their own church.

According to an interview that Rose-Marie Strach had with Gust, a meeting of the Greek business men was called. The meeting took place in Gus Bruskas' Liberty Café on Central Avenue. They debated the pros and cons of establishing the house as a church. After many hours and meetings and careful deliberation, the Greek business men reached an agreement. They would purchase the Raynolds' house and convert it temporarily into a church. Finally, there would be a church for the Greek community of Albuquerque.

The men traveled around the state in search of support. They went to Santa Fe, Las Vegas, Raton, Roswell, Grants, Gallup, Carlsbad and even to Trinidad, Colorado requesting donations to help in the purchase the entire block, which included the house and two lots in the adjacent back block facing Elm Street. They raised $12,562.07.

Helen Tricoglou describes it "as being a beautiful and large ranch-style home, with a nice grassy back yard where we had many outings and picnics." The yard was also described as having "a Garden of Eden-like atmosphere with luscious grapes, vegetables, trees and plants being in abundance. The vibrant color of green abounded." In the book *Huning's Highland Addition Neighborhood Walking Tour and Armchair Guide*, revised by Ann and Jim Carson, the Carsons describe the house as follows:

> Raynolds' mansion stands (stood) behind the cast stone wall that encircles it. The house was a brick structure nearly 150 feet long. It was built in the shape of an elongated "H," wooden porches filled in the east and west sides to make a rectangle. The house was built around 1907.

No good photo of the exterior has been found. The photo below is the only one found that shows the exerior of the Raynolds' house. It is "cast stone" made by Angelo DeTuillio as is the wall that surrounded the property and still does. The drawing on the next page was done from memory, but there are some deviations. Note in the drawing, that the windows on the north and south end of the house are different from those seen in the photo. The sketch shows the windmill in the back yard which was used to pump water up to be used in the house and yard.

Procession in front of the Albuquerque St. George Greek Orthodox Church. Photograph by William Laskar.

Drawing of Raynolds house on High Street. Drawing courtesy of Ruth Gannaway.

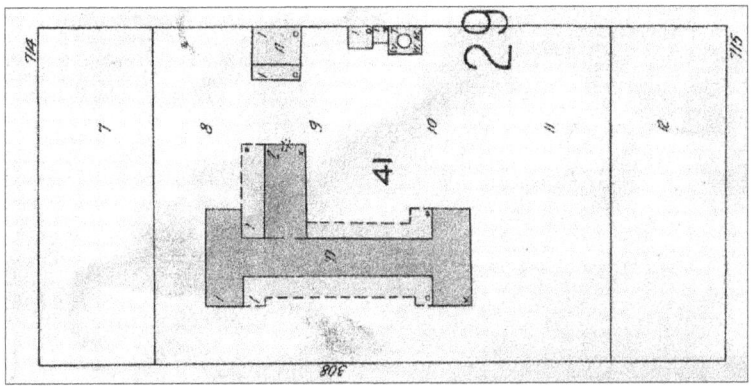

Interior plan of Raynolds' house.

According to the warranty deed, Jack Raynolds sold the property to the Hellenic Community of New Mexico.

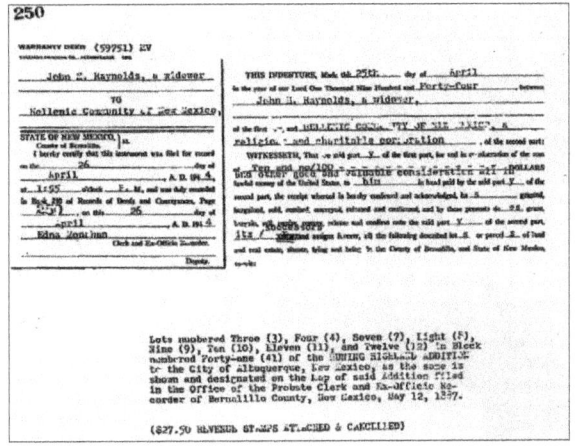

Warranty deed.

A number of changes needed to be made to convert the Raynolds' house into the church as can be seen in the following photo. The entrance to the church was on the northwest side of the front porch. The *Naos* or Nave, the main body of the church, was formally the Raynolds living room. In the photo, one can view the *Iconostasis* or Icon Stand,, which was built at the south end of the Nave (living room) and separated the Nave from the Sanctuary. The *Iconostasis* has three openings: the center door known as the Holy Door, and the doors on either side known as the Deacon's Doors. The Sanctuary, viewed in back of the *Iconostasis* is the area around the *Ieron* or Altar. The *Exapteryga* or metallic banners are visible behind the *Ieron*. Hanging in front of the *Iconostasis* is the *Kandeli* or the lantern candle holder. The photo is of the baptism of Angeline Mazas in 1946. Notice the galvanized tub which was used as the baptismal font.

Baptism in the Albuquerque St. George Greek Orthodox Church. Left to right: Father Sakellariou, Katherine Pomonis, Tom Pomonis, Angeline Mazas, Unknown Male, Steve Spondouras, Diamond Peterson (in back), and young Louis Karvelas.
Photograph by William Laskar

The building was used not only as a church, but also as a residence for the priest and his family and as a community hall. When the church Nave was used as a community hall for a party, a curtain was drawn across the *Iconostasis*. Connie Pouls said that the large room on the south side of the building behind the Ieron or Altar, which had been the Raynolds bedroom, had partitions removed and was used as a meeting room for different organizations and as the location for Sunday School. Exiting east out of the room, one entered a long hallway where the men and women's bathrooms were located to the right. The long hallway was a glassed-in solarium that faced the back yard. There were trap doors in the solarium and the kitchen that led to the basement, which housed a monstrous boiler that heated the entire house. Connie said "It was dark and the kids didn't want to have anything to do with it. The church didn't have any money so they made their own candles — in the basement."

Reverend Daniel Sakellariou came to Albuquerque in October, 1944, with his wife Ethel and daughters, Faye and Jenny. He organized the first Greek Orthodox Church in New Mexico, which included the El Paso parish. He was born at Pyrgos, Greece in 1888 and came from a family of clergymen and church laymen. At eighteen, he went to Palestine to engage in church work, then came to America two years later. Soon he entered the theological seminary in Chicago. He was ordained a priest in 1924 and died in 1966 in San Angelo, Texas (Jenny Sakellariou, personal communication.).

According to the Treasurers' Ledger, his salary was $200 per month. Jenny described the house as follows: "Our portion of the house included the Raynolds dining room as our living room and dining room with a small office for Father. Doors to the kitchen were closed to the church and opened for the many dinners and fund-raisers along the porch area which mother, the *Philoptochos* ladies and youth groups planned and helped." There was a second floor, above the kitchen, with two bedrooms, one for the girls and the other for Father and *Presvitera* (Greek title of honor for the priest's wife.). There was also a bathroom. They had no furniture and started buying some little by little with the money donated to Father Sakellariou. Their son, Andreas, was in the United States Air Force and after the war he came to stay with them for a while, but eventually went off to Texas A & M where he studied architecture.

Connie Pouls recalls a large kitchen "like you couldn't believe." This large kitchen was the area they did all the cooking for parties and celebrations. She thought the floor was going to fall in when they danced in the main room, the Nave, "You could see the floor wobbling up and down." One must be reminded that this house was built around 1907. Below is the only photo found taken of a community activity inside of the church.

The first service in the church was authorized by Archdiocese *Athenagoras* and held on October 15, 1944, officiated over by Reverend D. Sakellariou.

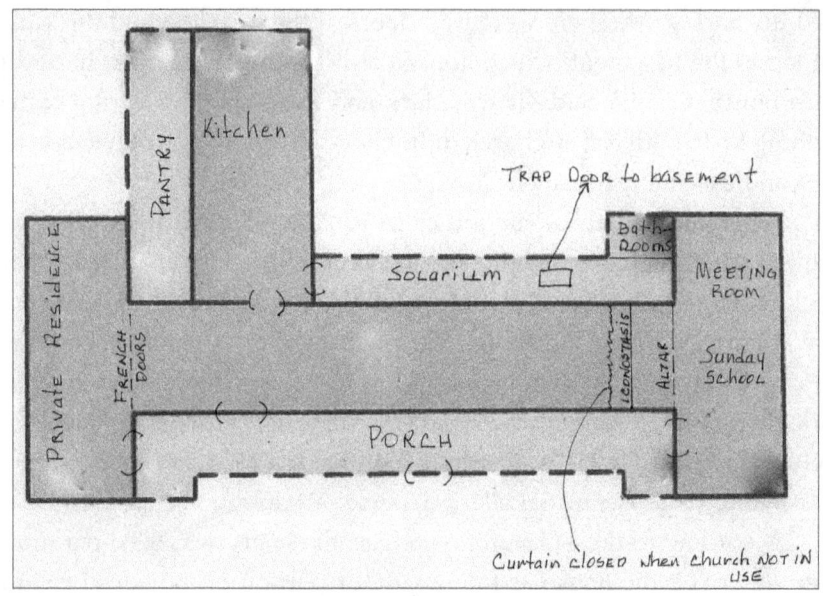

Floor plan of the Albuquerque St. George Greek Orthodox Church.

Celebration of Greek Independence Day. Photograph by William Laskar.

Reverend D. Sakellariou.
Photograph by William Laskar.

For 25 years, Mike Hontas was the *psalti* or chantor. Other psaltis included: Charles Moskos, Harry Pavlides, Them Thalas, Charles Askitas, John Gillis and G. Christakos.

The first choir director, a volunteer, was Jim Hontas. In 1946, Charles Askitas became choir director and was paid $40 a month through 1948. Akitas was replaced by Joseph W. Grant.

Jenny also said that Christine Pappas and Faye organized the choir in 1944. They started with ten members. None knew how to read Greek! Faye translated the liturgy into English and wrote it phonetically; some of the pages were typed and others were handwritten. The sheets were bound with black covers to make them look like books. The first members included: Georgia Assimakis, Christine Pappas, Pavlantos daughters, Jenny and Faye Sakellariou, Helen Tufares, Christine Tufares, Barbara Vrattos, and Tulla Zavakos

Jenny and Faye Sakellariou, Jamie May and Barbara Vrattos played the organ. It was an old pump organ with an opening on the side where Nick Kapnison would pump it to keep it working, as did Demo Pappas.

Sunday school teachers were: Helen Morris, who organized it and was the first teacher, Niki Janetakos, Effie Demas, Bessie Keller, Helen Chirigos, Helen Konougres, Tula Zavakos, Sofia Kartsotis, Helen Laris, Jennis Pavlantos, Soteria Meares, Presvitera Remoundos, and Mary Demas. Demetra (Tula Zavakos) said that she had brought her Sunday school books when she came from Ohio and they used them in Albuquerque. Their aim was to teach religious truth, chiefly through the use of Bible.

First Choir of the St. George Greek Orthodox Church. Photograph by William Laskar.

Greek School at the St. George Greek Orthodox Church. Photograph by William Laskar.

Greek school was taught by Fifi Vrattos. Mrs. Vrattos married widower Louis Vrattos (her maiden name was *Hrisanthakopoulou* and her first marriad name was *Kordoyannis*). Fifi was born in 1906 in *Gargayanni* and died in 2007 at 101 years. She is remembered as being a very hard, but a good teacher.

Victoria Poulos Moskos recalls one time during Greek School, while it was still in the first church, seeing whiffs of smoke coming up through the floor. Fifi would not let the pupils leave the classroom. As the smoke continued to come up from the basement, fortunately Fire Station No.2 across the street was called. When the firemen entered the building, they were shocked that the students were still at their seats afraid to move because of Fifi. They ordered an immediate evacuation. The firemen determined that someone (probably a Greek school student) had been playing around in the basement and started the fire. Damage was minor.

However, there is another side to this story as told to me by Connie Pouls. Gus Kirikos and Connie entered the basement through the infamous trap door and Gus brought out his matches so that they could see. At that moment the boiler went off with a big PHOO PHOO PHOM! They flew out of the basement, Gus dropped the match and it landed in a box of candles. They went to class and Fifi started smelling and seeing smoke come up through the boards. Fifi started yelling "R-o-o-o-n for your lives. The fire! The fire! Quick! The firemen across the street!" Ah, Connie and Gus, what a pair you were!

Connie (Constantina), the daughter of Olga and Charles Pouls, has many memories of the early community and the church. She recalls that during one of their classes they were learning about the patron saints. So, during recess, she and Gus (Constantino) Kirikos decided, "Oh this is neat. Is the dragon going to kill St. George or St. George is going to kill the dragon? We didn't have a spear or a horse, but that's okay. There were two flag poles. The one flag pole had the eagle and Gus decided that was going to be his spear and I decided to be the dragon." He chased her down the nave of the church. At the north end was a door with a glass top painted white the same color as the door. Connie opened the door and ran through it, closing it behind her. The spear went through the glass top as Father Remoundos was getting ready to open the door! "Constantino, Constantina come here." Charles Pouls laughed hysterically when he was told, and pulled out his wallet and said "Just go get a new glass, for Pete's sakes they are just kids. They were just playing St. George and the Dragon."

Starting around 1947, plans were underway for a new church. It was to be built in the Byzantine style, just north of the Raynolds' house.

Bishop *Athenagoras* pays a visit to assist in the planning of the church, circa 1945. Photograph by William Laskar.

On August 15, 1948, the first liturgy in the new church was celebrated by Reverand Silas Koskinas. Charles Moskos remembers Reverand Silas Koskinas, who was the priest from 1946 to 1949, as a gentle ascetic and who was later raised to the bishopric.

On July 1, 1949, Reverend Father Remoundos replaced Father Koskinas. Charles Moskos remembers Rev. Petros Remoundos as a bear of a man, who tempered religious solemnity with perceptive wit. He was the priest from 1949 to 1953.

The consecration of the church occurred on November 2, 1952 and was officiated by Bishop *Athenagoras*. It was given the name St. George Greek Orthodox Church because of the original efforts of George Ades and for St. George the *Tropaioforos*. Assisting the Bishop was Father Petros Remoundos. A banquet was held that night celebrating the consecration.

A committee was appointed to plan for the 1952 Consecration Celebration of the new church. The committee included: Peter N. Chumbris, General Chairman. The Committee for the Consecration Journal: Theo Karvelas, Father Remoundos and William Petropolous. The Committee of Finance included: Dorothy Kapnison, Chairman, Jamie May, Secretary and Georgia Kirikos, President of the Local Chapter of Philoptochos. The

Committee of Publication included: Bessie Keeler, Chairman; Effie Demas and Kay Preston. General Committee included: Louis Kanavos, Steve Karman, Gus Demas, Gust (Pa) Capel, William Kirikos, Angelo Mazas, Niki Janetakos, Fannie Assimakis, Sotrea Meares, Fontini Mavromatis, Helen Marhur, Jeanette Tufares, Jim Johnson, George Mavromatis, Pete Bruskas and Bessie Anthony.

> **OFFICIAL PROGRAM**
> **St. George's Greek Orthodox Church**
> **Consecration Ceremony**
>
> HIS GRACE, BISHOP ATHENAGORAS
> OFFICIATING
>
> Rev. Peter Remoundos, Assisting
>
> 308 High Street SE
> Albuquerque, N. M.
>
> Sunday, November 2, 1952, 9:00 A.M. to 2:00 P.M.
>
> The Great Vesper of the Relics
> Saturday, November 1, 1952, 7:30 P.M.
>
> DEDICATION DINNER PROGRAM
>
> Nov. 2, 1952, 7:00 P.M., Knights of Columbus Hall
>
> Toastmaster............................Peter N. Chumbris
> Invocation...............................Bishop Athenagoras
>
> ADDRESSES
> Rev. Peter Remoundos
> Rabbi David Shor
> His Grace, Bishop James E. Stoney
> His Excellency, Archbishop Edwin V. Byrne
> His Grace, Bishop Athenagoras

Program for the 1952 Consecration of the Albuquerque St. George Greek Orthodox Church.

By 1957, the needs of the community had grown and the first St. George Church was torn down to make way for a community hall. The new Community Center was completed in 1958.

In 1964, the bank loan with the First National Bank of Albuquerque was settled.

St. George Greek Orthodox Church, Albuquerque, New Mexico.
Photograph by Yorgos Marinakis.

Attendees at the St. George Greek Orthodox Church Consecration.
NOTE: Raynold's house to the right of the photo. 1952. Photograph by William Laskar.

Burning of the bank loan. Left to right: Peter Kostas, Clyde Hill (First National Bank President), Peter Bruskas, Angelos Gineris, Reverend George W. Arseniu and Gus Bruskas.

In the *Albuquerque Tribune* dated July 7, 1972, the headline read "Greek Church Leader Visited Albuquerque 3 times":

> Patriarch *Athenagoras* I, leader of the 126 million member Orthodox Church died in an Istanbul hospital early today. He was 86. He had visited Albuquerque three times while serving as Greek Orthodox Archbishop of North and South America. Mrs. Steve Anthony described him as "a wonderful man who would do anything for you. He took time out to visit the cemetery and pray for all the Greek people who had died."

The cemetery Mrs. Anthony was talking about was Fairview Cemetery on Yale Avenue. Those forgotten early Greeks buried in the old part also may have been blessed by Patriarch *Athenagoras*.

12

The Ledger: The Church's Financial History

It is fortunate that the St. George Greek Orthodox Church Treasure's Ledger still exists because it contains a wealth of information. Recorded in it are all the financial transactions from March 1944 to February 1953, (however it does skip 1949 through 1951). The treasurer in 1944 was Louis Vrattos. He recorded the names of the Greeks in Albuquerque, many towns in New Mexico, and Pueblo, Colorado, who contributed money (and their amounts) towards the purchase of the Raynolds' property. There were also companies and individuals who contributed who were not Greek. These were American Furniture, New Mexico Tile Co., Houser Farmacy! (Pharmacy), and Stromberg Clothing, to name just a few. In all, 150 names and companies are listed with donations totaling $12,56.07 ($161,613 in 2011 dollars).

The St. George Greek Orthodox Church Treasurer's Ledger. Photograph by Yorgos Marinakis.

Ledger page showing donations beginning March 1944 for the purchase of the Raynolds' property. Photograph by Yorgos Marinakis.

In April 1944, a document authorizing the purchase of the property was drawn up and signed by the acting board of trustees which was comprised of President, Gus Bruskas; Board of Directors: William Kirikos, James Frangos, John Carll, Louis Vrattos, George J. Giann, Cost Kikas, Helen Morris, John Benakis, Gust Ellis. Attested by Steve J. Spondiris, Secretary.

> unanimous vote of the total number of directors of the corporation.
>
> BOARD OF DIRECTORS:
> *[signature]* PRESIDENT
> William Pirikkos
> James Frangos
> John Cavell
> Louis Vrattos
> George J. Giann
> Curt Kerlks
> Helen Morris
> John G. Benakis
> *[signature]*
>
> ATTEST:
> Steve J. Spouduris, SECRETARY
>
> Document Authorizing Purchase of Property

Signatures authorizing the purchase of the Raynolds property.

The Ledger tells us the following story:

April 10, 1944, $1,000 was paid to Jack Raynolds as a deposit for the High Street property.

April 19, 1944, an additional $9,000 was paid to Jack Raynolds for total payment of $10,000 for the High Street property.

April 21, 1944, St. George Greek Orthodox Church was accepted for incorporation under the Laws of the State of New Mexico. Under the Articles of Incorporation, a formal Board of Trustees was formed.

April 1944, the Hellenic Community of New Mexico mortgaged 308 High Street to George Ades for $15,000. See Mortgage Deed.

Ledger entries showing payment to Jack Raynolds for his house.
Photograph by Yorgos Marinakis.

April 1944, *The Hellenic Community of New Mexico* was officially accepted and chartered by the Greek Orthodox Archdiocese of North and South America and the first priest was assigned.

April 1944, Reverend Daniel Sakellariou, was given $125 ($1,608 in 2011 dollars) for travel expenses. His monthly salary was $200 a month ($2,573 in 2011 dollars). Gust Pappas, the janitor, was paid $50 a month.

October 15, 1944, with the authorization of the Archdiocese, Reverend Sakellarious conducted the first service in the building. $228.20 was collected.

October 15, 1944, the first baptism was performed for Laskaris.

October 22, 1944, the first wedding was performed for Bob Katson.

October 26, 1944, the first funeral was performed for Tony Maryol.

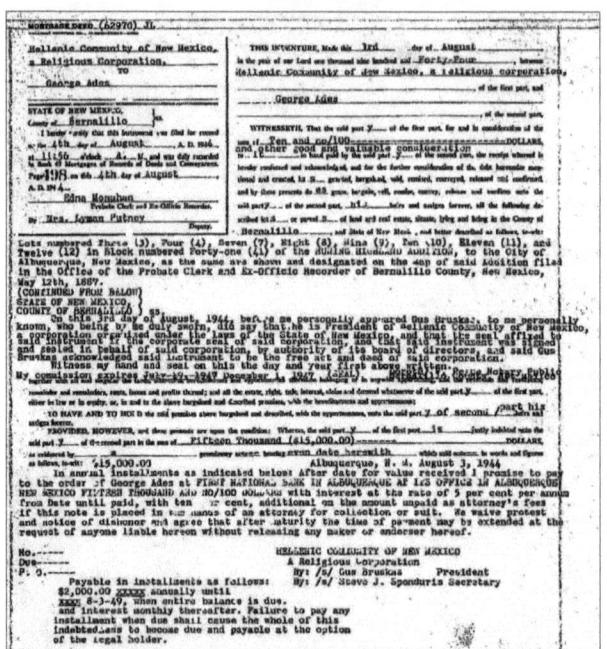

Mortgage Deed.

Expenditures for 1944 were: Payments to Raynolds, salaries, travel expenses, two torches, desk, chairs, boiler to make candles, wax, freight for chairs, choir books made by Father Sakellarious and daughters, yard maintenance, printing, repayment to Carll ($500), Bruskas ($500), and Ellis ($650) for loans, rental on the Knights of Columbus Hall, insurance, County Abstract, house improvements, *Thimiato* or *a* censor and freight, shades and linoleum, wall paper, plumbing, carpet cleaning, electrical work, paint, labor, taxes, school chairs, school supplies, Albuquerque Foundry and Mach., bank charges, and office expenses: Totaling $16,857.08 ($216,869 in 2011 dollars).

Income for 1944 was: Donations from the Greek community totalling $12,562.07, sale of a lot for $1,000, dues, baptisms, weddings, funerals, and memorial fees, door collection, donations, collections from Santa Fe and Las Vegas, donations for *Ikonas* or Icons: Totaling $20,925.41 ($269,205 in 2011 dollars) with a balance on hand in the bank $4,068.33.

In 1945, from February through June, a Second Building Drive took place. The towns in New Mexico and Colorado that contributed were:

Albuquerque $2,047; Grants $675; Gallup $820; Carlsbad $105; Las Vegas $275; Clovis $3,400, Roswell $540; Santa Fe $3,225; Taos $100; Raton $1,075 and Trinidad, Colorado $100. A special collection was set up to purchase the Icons, money was donated by Mrs. Alexandra Carrigan (mother of Helen Morris) to purchase the *Evanghelion* or Bible. An organ was rented. The first payment of $2,000 wasd made out to George Ades on January 30 towards the $15,000 ($192,978 in 2011 dollars) mortgage. In March, Reverend Sakellarious' salary war raised to $250 and Gust Pappas' to $60. The second payment of $2,000 was paid to George Ades on April 5. The *Kandili* or lantern candleholder arrived COD. The *Exapteryga* or metallic banner arrived COD also. Easter fell in May of that year and they bought flowers for the *Kouvouklion* or Christ's bier. Charles Pouls donated the *Epitaphion* or the cloth icon of the dead Christ was placed in the *Kouvouklion*. The community had an Easter party that year and lamb purchased from the Liberty Café and other groceries from Nick Kessanaidies. By June, Gust Pappas was no longer a janitor and replaced by Gus Fellis. November 21, they paid George Ades $2,000 and more improvements made on the house totalled $1,100. George Ades, was paid $2,000 on November 21 and $8,000 on November 28. Total amount paid to Ades was $16,000, which included interest.

Kouvouklion or Christ's bier. Left to right: Father Sakellariou, Georgia Benakis, Georgia Assimakis and unknown male. Photograph by William Laskar.

In 1946, George Ades executed a release of mortgage of $15,000 for the property which had been paid back to him by the Hellenic Community of Albuquerque.

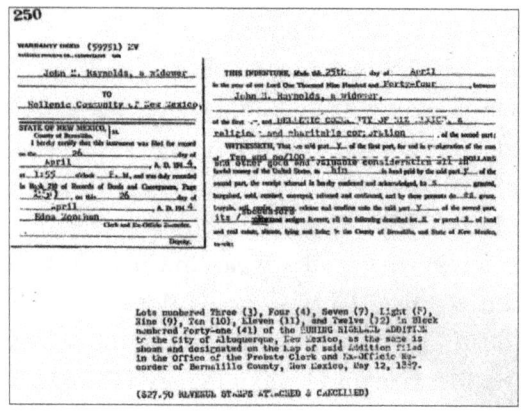

Release of Mortgage.

In 1946, a bank loan of $50,000 with the First National Bank of Albuquerque was taken out to pay for the new church the community was to have built.

July 1946, Reverend Silas Koskinas was designated by the Archdiocese to replace Reverend D. Sakellariou due to unfortunate circumstances.

July 1946, Reverend Silas Koskinas was paid $275 a month.

The Balance Sheet for 1946: Building Fund $1,626.95; Bonds $10,375; Bank balance on Jan. 1, 1947 was $15,231.07.

March 27, 1948 Honor of laying the cornerstone for the new church was given to Angelo Mazas, biggest contributor ($300), to the cornerstone project. Because of this contest, they were able to raise $19,867.70.

According to the Ledger, plans for the new church started around 1945 contacting an architectural firm and a surveyor.

Nov. 1945: Brittele and Ginner was paid $500.
Jan. 1946: Rose Beyer, Engineer, Surveying Firm, was paid $25.00.
Feb. 1946: Brittele and Ginner was paid $418.
Jan. 1947: Bittele and Ginner was paid $720.
Apr. 1948: Gayle Dellinger, Contractor, was paid $5,588.57.

Apr. 1948: Western Artist Monument was paid $60.
May 1948: Gayle Dellinger, Contractor, was paid $7,494.89.
June 1948: Gayle was paid $6,004.27.
July 1948: Gayle was paid $9,850.14.
Aug. 1948: Gayle was paid 5,929.20.
Sept. 1948: Gayle was paid 6,000.23.
Oct. 1948: S.Hyghtower was paid $873.70.
Oct. 1948: Gayle was paid $2,825.00.
Nov. 1948: S. Korber was paid $273.94.
Dec. 1948: Brittele Electric was paid $630.34.

Laying the cornerstone. Photograph by William Laskar.

The total amount documented in the Ledger to build St. George Greek Orthodox Church of Albuquerque was $47,193.28.

December 1948, Bank balance $149.00.

There were no recordings in the Ledger from 1948 to 1952. In 1948, Louis Vrattos, the treasurer, was elected president of the Hellenic Community with Steve Kaplanidis replacing him. This may be the reason there were no recordings in the Ledger during this period. Was there another Ledger started? If so, where is it? Recordings began again in 1952 through 1953.

July 1, 1949 Father Remoundos replaced Father Koskinas.

In 1952, the Church was consecrated. Expenses for the consecration service were as follows:

Ad book $4,826.20 which was probably the printing of the Consecration Album, keys $1,105, oil $1,001, banquet $1,167 and donations $600.

13

The Greek Organizations

The Greeks organized numerous fraternal and social organizations as they were reluctant to relinquish their heritage of which they were very loyal. These ethnic clubs brought Greeks with similar beliefs together and helped them make friendships in their new community. The parties were important assuring continuation of awareness of their culture, music and their language. The Greek organizations in Albuquerque were the National AHEPA Organization (American Hellenic Education Progressive Association), the *Philoptochos,* the Daughters of Penelope, and the GOYA (Greek Orthodox Youth of America), and to some extent, Greek Coffee Houses. To find information on each of the organizations, I researched their websites. For the names of those Greeks who were members in these organizations in Albuquerque, I also researched the 1952 Consecration Album, New Mexico obituaries, New Mexico death certificates, and New Mexico newspaper clippings.

American Hellenic Education Progressive Association (AHEPA)

History

This fraternal organization was founded on July 26, 1922 "in response to the evils of bigotry and racism that emerged in early 20th century American society." It helped Greek immigrants assimilate into society. Its founders were George Polos and John Angelopoulos. Today, AHEPA brings the ideals of ancient Greece, which includes philanthropy, education, civic responsibility, and family and individual excellence, to the community. Although a majority of the membership is composed of Americans of Greek descent, application for membership is open to anyone who believes in the mission of the organization.

It is the largest and oldest fraternal American-based, Greek heritage grassroots membership organization. It was the first national organization to lead the crusade for naturalization among immigrants.

A Brother AHEPAN, President Roosevelt

The Mission

"AHEPA desires to promote Hellenism, Education, Philanthropy, Civic Responsibility, and Family and individual Excellence."

The first AHEPA Organization in the western United States was formed circa 1931 and included the states of New Mexico, Colorado, Wyoming, parts of Texas, and Arizona.

Listed below are the names of the first Albuquerque Ahepans:
George D. Ades, Chris Christopoulou, Peter Theodoratos, James Ipiotis, Anthony Pavlantos, Robert Katson, Nick John Matsoukas, George Giann (Gianopouloos), Gus Bruskas, James Bruskas, Peter Bruskas, Panagiotes Arvanitakis, William Assimakis, John Benakis, John C. Capels, "Pa" Capels, James Chrisafie. Daniel L. Askos, George Pavlantos, Paul Drake, Louis Chalamides, George Chalamides, Roy Chalamides, John Chirigos, John Collaros, Gus Daskalos, Gus Ellis (Eliopoulos), James Frangos, Mike

Hontas, William Janetakos, Kosta (Cost) Kakis, Panos Karvelas, Stratis Kaplanides, Paul Kapnison, William Kirikos, Charles (Constantino) Pouls, Tom Nick Manole, Photios Moskos, Nick John Matsukas, George May, Tom Mays, William Meares, George Nichols, Aristites Pappas, Anthony Pappas, Nick George Pappas, James Pavlakos, Sam (Sarantos) Pavlakos, Theodore Pavlantos, George Petropolis, George G. Poulos, Paul Psaltis, William Psaltis, Louis Samaras, Steve Sponduris, and Paul Symon.

In the *Albuquerque Journal*, dated June 18, 1936, V. I. Chebithe, of New York and the Supreme President of AHEPA stated at the district convention in Santa Fe, that the Greeks in America have four major problems:

> To find Greek wives for Greeks and Greek husbands for Greek women; to educate Americans to understand the Greeks; to educate the Greeks to understand Americans and American customs; to extend educational facilities of all kinds for Greek people.

He went on to say AHEPA was trying to meet these problems by bringing Greeks together socially and for mutual benefit, and by inviting Americans to participate in their social and other functions. President Roosevelt was to be invited!

Hellenic Social Club 1923

In the *Albuquerque Journal*, dated March 23, 1923 there was an ad: "The Greek colony of Albuquerque has organized a club to be known as the Hellenic Social Club. The club has been granted a charter by the State Corporation Commission. George Stonas was manager and secretary, Jim Chrisofis was clerk."

An ad also appeared in the 1923 City Directory. "Hellenic Social Club at 108½ N. 4th. Geo Stonas., sec." It did not appear in the directory the following year. Was this a coffee-house or a *kaffenion*?

These coffeehouses were solutions to the newly arrived immigrants who were far from home and family. They provided companionship, entertainment where the men could sit and talk politics (vociferously), play cards and reminisce of their homeland. It served as a clearing-house for jobs and housing. Most importantly, it was a place where the uneducated Greek could get a letter from home read to him. However, gambling became a problem and many of these *kaffenions* were shut down.

Daughters of Penelope – Helen of Troy, Chapter No. 19

History

According to the AHEPA Silver District wed site "The Daughters of Penelope was the realization of Alexandra Apostollides Sonenfeld's dream. Her desire was to create a woman's organization and because of her perseverance and the encouragement of her husband, Dr. Emanuel Apostollides, a devoted AHEPAN, she formed Chapter #1, with 25 charter members on November 16th, 1919 in San Francisco, California." The Daughters became the first Greek-American women's organization in the United States.

At its onset here in New Mexico, Albuquerque and Santa Fe were one chapter and monthly meetings held alternately in each city.

The Daughters of Penelope received its chapter on October 1934 with 16 members. It became officially an auxiliary of the Order of AHEPA in 1939 and named Helen of Troy Chapter after one of their members, Helen Carrigan Morris, for her work in organizing the first chapter. She became its first president. Members of the first Albuquerque chapter included: Helen Morris, Anastasia Ipiotis, Fannie Pavlantos, Vera Pavlantos, Bessie Pavlantos, Helen Columbus, Anna Laskar, Anna Psalatis, Edith Carellas, and Mary Hotis.

The *Albuquerque Tribune* on January 25, 1942, ran a story about the Daughters of Penelope which read as follows: "The Penelope order has conducted civic and charitable projects during the past year. The group has purchased Defense Bonds and aided in patriotic programs. Holiday programs and gifts have been presented patients at the AHEPA National Tuberculosis Sanatorium here."

Members later included: Penelope Katson, Souris, Alexandra Kartas, Mary Daskalos, Helen Pomonis, Carmen Pomonis, Ethel Kalangis, Goldie Karones, Dorothy Ellis, Anna Hontas, Madeline Hontas, Angeline Hontas, Viola Spounduris, Christine Pappas, Ellen Tertipes, Helen and Julia Rakagis, Constance Demopoulos, Lela Chalamides, Helen Chirigos, Dorothy Kapnison, Georgia Kirikos, Olga Pouls, Jamie Bell May, Eunice Marie Mays, Angie Pappas, Stella Samaras, Stella Zavakos, Helen Marhur, Fannie Assimakis, Lorraine Bruskas, Jamie May, Pauline Benakis, Sotrea

Meares, Florence Provas, Angeline Pavlides, Renea Morris, Lorene Bruskas, Catherine Chalamidas, Jeanette Tufares, Helen Laris, Mary Daskalos, Honey Pavlides, Bessie Vrattos, Josephine Mazas, Goldie Poulos, and Mary Demas.

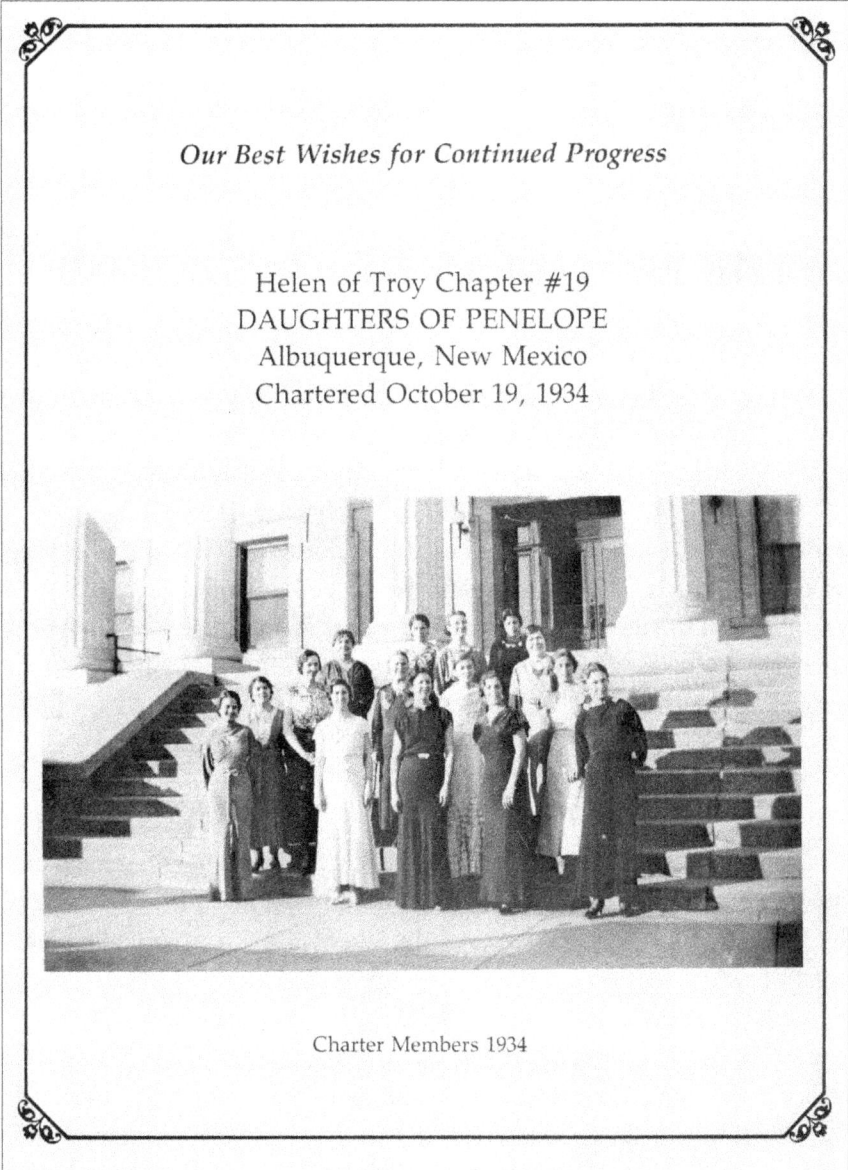

The first Daughters of Penelope of New Mexico.

Philoptochos

History

According to Stella Coumantaros in her article "The Greek Orthodox Ladies *Philoptochos* Society and The Greek American Community," in 1902 in New York, a small group of women met to form a philanthropic organization to assist the needy Greek family immigrants. They modeled the ideas for their organization after a group of well-to-do Greek Orthodox women refugees of Smyrna who fled the Turkish holocaust.

With the arrival of Archbishop *Athenagoras* in February 1931 to assume the leadership of the Greek Orthodox Church in North and South America, a new era began in the life and mission of the Greek Orthodox community.

The Thirties were turbulent times for the Greeks in America and Archbishop *Athenagoras* soon realized that there was an urgent need to provide philanthropic and relief services to the poor and suffering.

With the convening of the Fourth Archdiocesan General Assembly in New York City, in November, 1931, Archbishop *Athenagoras* urged the establishment of a national women's organization as the official philanthropic arm of the Church. The organization was to be known as *Philoptochos*. The Archbishop also asked that the Feast Day of Saints *Cosmas* and *Damianos*, which is observed on November 1st, be designated as the Patron Saints of *Philoptochos*."

The Mission

The Greek Orthodox Ladies' *Philoptochos* Society is the right hand of the Church. The Society's main mission is philanthropy and communal outreach. All Orthodox Christian women over the age of 18 who are members of the parish are strongly encouraged to become *Philoptochos* members. The first Presidents in Albuquerque, in chronological order, were: Lou Davis, Olga Pouls, Christine Pappas, Fannie Assimakis, Dorothy Kapnison, Rita Moskos, Voula Pappas, and Georgia Kirikos. Members were: Georgia Chalamides, Lela Chalamides, Helen Chirigos, Mary Collaros, Tula Columbus, Pauline Benakis, Anna Hontis, Jamie Bell May, Fotini Mavromatis, Sotria Meares, Helen Morris, Tasia Pappas, Angie Pappas, Stavroula N. Pappas, Rose

Psavlakos, Bessie Pavlantos Anthony, Helen Petropoulos, Goldie Poulos, Mary Symon, Christina Psaltis, Stella Zavakos, Jennie Pavlantos, Jeanette Tufares, Andonia Psachos and Helen Rakagis.

Angeline Pappas, who passed away July 15, 2008, was a charter member of *Philoptochos*. Her daughter, Elaine told me this story on October 13, 2008.

> When she was living in Chicago, Mom and her sisters were good friends with the priest Father *Athenagoras*. Every church, at that time, had their own women's auxiliary. Father *Athenagoras* went on to become a bishop and they remained friends. He was then elevated to Archbishop of North and South America. When he was visiting Chicago, my aunts and mother had him over for dinner. They were discussing their women's auxiliary and the Archbishop wondered why the women were not focused and united in their church work. He said they should be doing more than just helping the church. I am not sure when he came up with the title of *Philoptochos*, but he said all the auxiliaries should be called *Philoptochos* and that they should be helping their own communities and others. Mom's church auxiliary was the first to call themselves *Philoptochos* and those women went to other churches in Chicago to encourage them to join. When Mom moved to Dayton, Ohio, she got the Dayton women to change their name from Annunciation Auxiliary to *Philoptochos*. When mom moved to Albuquerque she found there was a St. George Woman's Auxiliary. Mom convinced the Albuquerque women to join the national *Philoptochos* and change their name. When Archbishop *Athenagoras* was passing through Albuquerque, he contacted Mom and she and many community members went to the Santa Fe Depot to welcome him in 1947.

Greek Orthodox Youth of America (GOYA)

When Archbishop Michael assumed leadership of the Church in North and South America, he helped the federations of youth groups unite on a national level in an organization named the Greek Orthodox Youth of America, or GOYA on July, 1951 and gave this talk at the 6th GOYA Conference in Los Angeles, July 15, 1957 entitled: "The Treasure of Archbishop Michael of North and South America."

As modern Americans of Greek descent you will accomplish much; but in attaining worldly destinies never forget that as members of GOYA, you who are our pride and hope belong to an essentially religious organization, and whatever you attain on this earth is, in the last analysis, of little value without a deep and firm belief in the tried and tested religion of your forefathers. Adhere firmly to this faith, observe strictly its tenets, and in so doing you will in fact realize the motto of GOYA and truly live your Orthodox faith, thus becoming better Christians and better American citizens worthy of your noble Greek descent. With all my blessing for the future, in the name of our Lord Jesus Christ.

Aims

To unite all Greek Youth of New Mexico. Participate in solution of problems confronting the church. Stress the importance of religion, family and civic life. Promote social and cultural activities. Perpetuate customs and traditions of the Greek Orthodox Church. Teach its membership the administration of a progressive community. Participate in worthwhile civic activities.

The president was Lieutenant Nick Zilson , Vice President James Demopoulos, Secretary Georgia Benakis. Board of Directors were John Mavromatis, Educational; Georgjean May Social; George Eleamos, Athletic and Father Remoundos, Advisor. Members included: Kula Rakagis, Betty Rakagis, Francis Rakagis, Barbara Vrattos, Helen Tufares, Nick Helaris, George Margelos, Bill Kardaras, Gus Logos, George Ragatin, Chris Demopoulos, Harry Carratt, John Mavromatis, Charles Moskos, George Argyres, Angie Hontas, Renia Morris and Gus Markos.

The play *Nostalgia* by Archbishop *Kavadas* was performed by the Hellenic Youth Club. It is a play about Odysseus and his 20 years of wanderings. The players were: Odysseus, George Argyros; Nymph, Angie Hontas, Goddess Athena, Helen Tufares; God Hermes, Zis Katsavis (back); Nymph, Tula Klenck; Sailor, Jim Hallick; Calypso, Barbara Vrattos; Sailor,

Nick Zilson, (back); Ismini, Carol Petropoulos; Kleio, Renia Morris (back); Mary Mavromatis; Elli, Georgia Benakis (back). The costumes designed by Mia Panos, a University of New Mexico student and made by Mrs. Angelo Mazas and Mrs. Dino Tufares. The scenery was constructed by John Lathorakis and Mia Panos and make-up was done by Georgjean May and Madaline Psaltis, Giberta Theodore, programs and Charles Moskos, tickets. Prompter was Louis Vrattos and the play was directed by Rev. Peter Remoundous.

Greek Youth of New Mexico in costume for the play *Nostalgia*.

The First Presidents of Albuquerque's St. George Greek Orthodox Community

The first Presidents of the Community were: 1944 Gus Bruskas; 1945 George Ades; 1946 Angelo Mazas; 1947 Gus Bruskas; 1948 Louis Vrattos; 1949 John Benakis; 1950 James Frangos; 1951 Paul Kapnison; and 1952 John Chumbris.

GEORGE ADES

ANGELO MAZAS

GUS BRUSKAS

PAUL KAPNISON

JAMES FRANGOS

JOHN BENAKIS

LOUIS VRATTOS

First Presidents of Albuquerque's St. George Greek Orthodox Community.

14

Greek-Americans In The Wars

The Greeks in the United States proudly served in the military. They responded enthusiastically to calls for volunteers in the armed forces during World War One. Greek families bought victory bonds estimated at $10 million. It is stated that this amount was the highest of any national group. The Greek men proclaimed their willingness to fight for the United States.

> We are, as a race, Greek, and will remain so, but America is our country, America is our home, our estate, our family, our church, our education, and everything we possess. Therefore, it is our holy duty to fight and protect our country which is our life.

U.S. Government Bond poster from World War One.

Many of the young Greek men volunteered to fight during World War One and became American citizen in so doing. My father, Tom (Anastasios) Pomonis, was one of them. Greek men of Albuquerque who became American citizens by serving in World War One were: John Goches, Mike Hontas, Stratis Kaplanides, Peter (Panos) Karvelas, George M. Leakon (Leakow), George Mavromatis, Paul Psaltis, Kostandinos Tufares, Louis Vrattos, and Peter Rallis (photo below). Possibly some of these men were veterans of the last two Balkan Wars and because the Greek government could not afford to pay for their passage back to Greece to fight for their country, they were given the alternative to serve the country they adopted.

Peter Rallis. Photograph courtesy of his son.

Other Greek men in Albuquerque who were drafted were: Gus James Alex, John Balascos, George Buras (George Bucus), meat cutter, George Stamat Chartos, James Dowlie (James Doules), cook, John Maskiotis (John Miskiostis), Tom Meihas, Pedro Nickolindakis, Philip Pappas, James William Provas, Terp Andros Smirnalos, Stelios (Samuel) S. Vasil and Philip Vouteretren (Venterice). It is not known what happened to these men.

The headlines of The Deming Headlight, October 11, 1918, read:

GREEKS IN U.S. ARMY NUMBER MORE THAN IN GREEK ARMIES
When this war is over and the statistics have all been compiled, it is certain that few, if any, foreign races in the United States will be able to show a higher record than the Greeks, not only for the proportion of their citizens who served in the war either in the Greek or the American armies, but also for their generosity in contributing to the different drives for patriotic and benevolent objects, for their patriotism, their discipline and obedience.

World War Two brought a new surge of patriotism from the Greek community. During World War Two, the U. S. Treasury Department gave AHEPA the special privilege of selling war bonds. They sold a half a billion dollars worth of war bonds! The Greek-Americans also stated that, more than ever, "this war is our war and its financing is our problem, too." Charles Moskos wrote, "The war effort became a matter that combined Greek ethnic pride and American patriotism."

The AHEPA expanded their activities into Red Cross campaigns, a national war chest campaign, the civilian defense campaign, blood donations, hospital visitations and helping in the preparation of Red Cross supplies. The American Red Cross designated March 25, 1943, as Greek Day in honor of all the help that AHEPA had provided. Connie Pouls remembers her mother Olga Pouls, Bessie Pavlantos and several other Greek ladies going down to the corner of 4th and Central Avenue setting up tables and selling baklava. The money they made paid for the purchase of war bonds. Many Greek women of Albuquerque did their part by rolling bandages and sewing garments for the Red Cross. The children were given 10¢ each week which they used to buy war bonds at school.

It is estimated that 60,000 Greek-Americans served with the armed forces in World War Two. They served proudly and some lost their lives.

Three of Gus "Pop" Capels sons fought in World War Two. William in Persia, Jimmy in Germany and John, who was killed during the invasion of Normandy is buried in Epinal, France.

George Janos, son of Alex Janos, reported missing September 6, 1943. The War Department informed his father that he left England on a bombing flight and did not return.

Jack Ellis, son of Gus Ellis died during the Bataan Death March in the Philippines.

Jim Argeanas, son of Theo and Angeliki Argeanas served in the United State Army and survived the Bataan Death March in the Philippines.

Andy Argeanas, son of Theo and Angeliki Argeanas served in the United States Army in South Africa and Europe.

George Argeanas, son of Theo and Angeliki Argeanas served in the United States Navy at the end of the War.

Samuel Bezos was a lieutenant in the United States Air Force.

John Collaros served as a tech sergeant in the United States Army Signal Corp. He was a radio telegrapher in Alaska monitoring the Japanese during the Pacific Theater. When John passed away in 1974, his wife Mary received a letter from General Gerald Ford commending him for his work during the war.

Steve Collaros served with the United States Army as a paratrooper in the Pacific Theater.

Miller Pavlides served in the United States Army as a Captain and received the Bronze Medal of Honor.

Theodore Pavlantos (left in photo) served in the United States Navy and was stationed at Pearl Harbor.

George Pavlantos (right in photo) was drafted at the age of 26 despite his marital status and served in the United States Navy.

Theodore and George Pavlantos.
Photograph courtesy of Mrs. Jenny Pavlantos.

William Gus Koulas, son of Gus and Sophie Koulas received his B.S. and M.A. Degrees from the University of New Mexico. He served in the United States Air Force. He founded the New Mexico Society of Professional Engineers and its magazine.

Nick Argos served in the Greek Army in Egypt during World War Two.

Konstantinos "Gus" Daskalos spearheaded the efforts and successes of the Greek War Relief Association (GWRA) during World War Two here in Albuquerque.

In his book *American Community in Transition*, Charles Moskos wrote:

> In the five-month interval between the Italian attack and the subsequent German occupation of Greece over $5 million in money and supplies were raised. Seven hundred thousand tons of food, clothing, and medicines were shipped to Greece on neutral Swedish vessels. It is estimated that a third of the Greek population were saved from death because of the efforts of the GWRA.

The Albuquerque Daughters of Penelope was one of only eight national chapters that remained active during World War Two. They held benefit teas and traveled throughout the state soliciting funds for the Greek War Relief.

Greeks stranded in Greece or living in Greece during the war relate their stories of hardships during those years. They all remember the hunger and cold that they endured, the death they saw and the terrible memories which are still etched in their minds.

Bessie Frangos came from Peristasis and tells her story of her early life in Greece during World War Two. She and a friend were playing near the sea when a torpedo came up onto the beach. She remembers how her father had been very protective of his family during those war years.

Maria Gregorios Petropoulos Argyres came from Kalamata. She tells the story of her time in Greece during World War Two when the Germans took her father to a concentration camp. They told her mother that if she had money to give them the Germans would help her find him. She sold all the electrical wiring and whatever else in the house, but they never found him.

Gus Hantzopoulos came from Ana Hora, Nafpaktos and tells his story of life in Greece during World War Two. When he was 12, he left his home with his father to look for work and walked for two days. It was April and there was snow on the ground; his shoes were old and the toes were out, so he put rags on his feet so they wouldn't get frost bit. Nearing *Messolongi*, he and his father encountered an Italian convoy coming from Epirus. The men in the convoy started making fun of them and laughing. The road was narrow and they swerved their trucks trying to hit him and his father. He and his father ran and jumped into a ditch. Otherwise he felt they would have killed them.

Mary Mavromatis Pavlides, stranded with her mother and siblings in Athens during the war, relates the horror she experienced.

> We went through very bad times, a lot of hardship—unbelievable. The German occupation forces actually went out of their way to be brutal. People, dead people on the street, from starvation. We would go out on the sidewalks and we could see the corpses rotting and they could stay there for a week before they would pick them up. We sold everything we had. My mother sold her jewelry she had so that we could survive. The worse thing I have ever seen in my whole life—and I hope I never see it again—was a big pickup truck full of parts of bodies—heads, legs, arms—I started screaming—I was just a young girl then...I...I...will never forget that!

The Swedish liner *Gripsholm*, acting as a relief ship, arrived in Jersey City, New Jersey, on August 2, 1945, carrying 1,496 passengers from India and Greece, Mary (Mavromatis) Pavlides and her family were met by her father George Mavromatis after many years of separation.

During the Korean War, 1950–1953, many of the young men of the new generation participated.

John Theo Argeanas, son of Mrs. Angeline Argeanas served in the Navy for a year in Korea on the *U.S.S. St. Paul*.

Mike Argeanas, son of Theo and Angeliki Argeanas, served in Korea from 1946 to 1948.

Deno Benakis, son of John and Pauline Benakis served in the United States Navy on the *U.S.S. McGowan* in Korea.

Kostantinos G. Hadjidakis served in the United State Army during the Korean War. He received his Master's Degree using the G.I. Bill and later worked for the Corp. of Engineers and NASA.

Louis P. Karvelas, son of Peter and Angelika Kaarvelas, served for two years in the United States Army from 1952 to 1954 and was stationed at Fort. McClellan, Alabama, the US Army Chemical School.

Chris Kirikos, son of William and Georgia Kirikos, served in the Army Infantry for 23 years touring many countries in Europe and Asia.

Dean Pappas, son of Anthony and Angeliki Pappas, served as a Colonel in the United States Air Force and upon retirement, worked for Hewlett Packard.

Charles Psachos, son of Mr. and Mrs. Chris Psachos, served in the U. S. Army.

John A. Theodore served in the Navy starting in 1949, and in Korea from 1951 to 1952 in the 1st Marine Air Wing.

Socrates C. Zavakos, son of Stella Zavakos, served in the U. S. Navy on the *U.S.S. Bryce Canyon.*

During the Viet Nam War, 1963-1974, several of our young men of the new generation participated.

Demetrios Pappas was in the United State Army as a dentist at Fort Sill, Oklahoma from 1963-65.

Captain Peter J. Gineris stationed at El Paso, Texas. He died of injuries sustained in an airplane accident near Mount Taylor in 1961 during the Vietnam War.

John Theo. Argeanas

John Argeanas, son of Mrs. Angeline Argeanas, is with the U. S. Navy stationed in Long Beach, California. John was in Korea for a year on the U.S.S. St. Paul. He is a gradute of Highland High School.

Deno Benakis

Deno Benakis, son of Mr. and Mrs. John Benakis, serves on the U.S.S. Gowan, has been in Korea since March, 1952. He attended University of New Mexico, affiliated with Kappa Sigma.

John A. Theodore

John A. Theodore, C.B.D. No. 1509, Navy No. 824, Transportation, c/o FPO, San Francisco, Calif. Entered Navy as Sea-Bee, June, 1949. Served at Guam 28 months 9 months in Korea from Aug. 1951, to May, 1952, with the 1st Marine Air Wing, and now serving at Kwajelin Island in Pacific.

Charles Psachos

Charles Psachos, son of Mr. and Mrs. Chris Psachos, is with the U. S. Army. Charles is stationed in England.

Nick Kapnison

Nick Kapnison, son of Mr. and Mrs. Paul Kapnison, is a graduate of Albuquerque High School. Nick is in the U. S. Army, stationed at Ft. Leonard Wood in Missouri. He attended Wentworth Military School, New Mexico A&M, and the University of New Mexico where he was a member of the Kappa Sigma Fraternity. He sang in our church choir for a number of years.

Socrates C. Zavakos

Socrates Zavakos, son of Mrs. Stella Zavakos, is with the U. S. Navy on the U.S.S. Bryce Canyon somewhere in Japan.

Louis Karvelas

Louis Karvelas, son of Mr. and Mrs. Peter Karvelas, was an honor graduate of the Massachusetts Institute of Technology. He was an honor graduate of Albuquerque High, winning a scholarship. He studied chemical engineering and business administration and graduated from M.I.T. with top honors in his class. He was a chemist with Du Pont Company at the H-bomb plant in Georgia. He is now stationed at F

Young Albuquerque Greek-Americans in the military.

15

The Post-War Generation

By the end of World War Two, the Greeks of Albuquerque were moving into newer neighborhoods and becoming part of mainstream America. They were solidly entrenched in the middle class. Their children had grown and many had gone off to college, married, and/or were running their father's business.

Mike Argeanas was the son of Theodore and Angelina Argeanas. He was the proprietor of an auto parts store in Albuquerque.

Tom Arvas is the son of Peter and Katherine Arvanitakis. He is a dentist.

Georgia Assimakis is the daughter of William and Fannie Assimakis. She graduated with high honors and awarded a nursing scholarship to the Regina School of Nursing.

Patricia Assimakis is the daughter of William and Fannie Assimakis. She is in real estate in California.

Helen (Frangos) Dountas is the daughter of James and Bessie Frangos. She is an Albuquerque Public Schools Educational Assistant.

Georgia Chalamidas was the daughter of Mr. and Mrs. Roy Chalamidas. She fell from a horse during a University of New Mexico riding class and died three hours later.

Evie (Chirigos) Bardas was the daughter of John and Helen Chirigos. She received a Master's Degree in English from University of New Mexico and taught for ten years. She became a Unitarian minister.

Michael D. Chirigos is the son of John and Helen Chirigos. He received his Master's Degree from University of New Mexico in park administration and worked for the City of Albuquerque Parks and Recreation.

Dean Chirigos is the son of John and Helen Chirigos. He received his degree from University of New Mexico in electrical engineering and worked for the City of Farmington.

Sophie Collaros is the daughter of John and Mary Collaros. She studied in Athens and became a conservator of antiquities and a teacher in Albuquerque.

James Demopoulos, son of Alex and Constance Demopoulos, became the proprietor of Unique Cleaners. The cleaning business was the same his father had been in.

Nick Kapnison, son of Paul and Dorothy Kapnison, has continued in his father's footsteps by running upscale Albuquerque restaurants. He was told by his aunt that the family was called *kapnistos*, or one who smokes, because his great grandfather had been in the tobacco business. Their real name was Pantagis.

Louis Karvelas, son of Peter and Angelica Karvelas, received a Bachelors of Science from MIT and an MBA from Harvard. He worked for Humble Oil Co. in Houston, Texas.

Chris Kirikos is the son of William and Georgia Kirikos. After retiring from the military and getting a business degree, he went into the same business his father had been. He is proprietor of Panza Llena Café.

Michael Kirikos is also the son of William and Georgia Kirikos. He is the proprietor of Kirikos Family Funeral Home in Truth or Consequences, New Mexico.

William Laskar was the son of Basil and Anna Laskurakis. He became a well-known photographer in Albuquerque and ran his own business known as Laskar Photo Service.

Renia Morris was the daughter of James and Helen Morris. She studied to become a teacher and eventually school administrator in California.

Harry Moskos (photo below, left) is the son of Charles and Rita Moskos. He worked for the Associated Press, and was promoted to Chief of the Bureau in Hawaii. He was City Editor and later Managing Editor of the *Albuquerque Tribune*.

Charles Moskos (photo below, right) was the son of Charles and Rita Moskos. He was a leading sociologist and professor at Northwestern University. He was the author of the book *Greek American, Struggle and Success*. Charles passed away in 2008.

Elaine Pappas is the daughter of Anthony and Angeliki Pappas. She is a graduate of San Diego State University with a Masters Degree in Education.

AnnaMaria Pappas is the daughter of Anthony and Angeliki Pappas. She is a graduate of Colorado State Univesity in Fort Collins with a Masters Degree in counseling.

Harry and Charles Moskos. Photograph courtesy of Charles Moskos.

Basil G. Pouls, son of Charles and Olga Pouls, is a graduate of the Massachusetts Institute of Technology. He was partners in Koogle and Pouls Engineering, Inc., in Albuquerque.

Constance Pouls, daughter of Charles and Olga Pouls has become a very talented iconographer.

Anna Psaltis is the daughter of Paul and Christina Psaltis. She sang leading roles in operas in Chicago.

William Pappas is the son of Gust and Christine Pappas. He became a Director for the Chicago Theater and the Canadian Theater, Toronto.

Demetrios Pappas is the son of Harry and Tessie Pappas. He is a graduate of Marquette University Medical School in Milwaukee, Wisconsin, and spent two more years specializing in pediatric dentistry.

Miller Pavlides was the son of Harry and Europa Pavlides. He was a Registered Public accountant and had his own business.

16

Another Patrida

In the late 1800s, the youth of Greece came to America in search of work. They helped build the United States' industry and business, its professions, politics, art and music, and provided the inexhaustible labor supply so necessary for America's phenomenal growth. Around the 1880s, they started coming to Albuquerque and stayed and became part of this land that so much reminded them of their *patrida* or birth place. They worked hard and eventually became business owners and homeowners. They served in the United States military and became United States citizens. They loved this country. They brought their church and religion here freely and raised their children to appreciate their heritage.

This is the story of the Greeks in Albuquerque starting around 1880 through 1952. They assimilated into the United States and contributed to Albuquerque's ethnic and cultural diversity. This country gave them opportunity, and in turn, they gave their best.

He couldn't believe his eyes, the sky was blue, like the color of the flag from his homeland. And the clouds were magnificent as they hung over the mountains and reached into the sky. They reminded him of those near his village in the Peloponnese. There were sheep grazing in the fields…just like home.

Home—Greece—thousands of miles away—but here in New Mexico—he has found another Greece.

He had left Chicago ten days ago. Crowded, noisy and gray. Chicago, where doctors had told him that he had TB and must go West—to a strange land or he will die there in Chicago—alone!

Some did die, alone, and others survived and began a new life in the land that so much reminded them of their patrida—New Mexico.

The Sandia Mountains. Photograph by Yorgos Marinakis.

Selected Bibliography

Brewer, David. *The Greek War of Independence,* 2001.

Burgess, Thomas. *Greeks In America: An Account of Their Coming, Progress, Customs, Living and Aspirations,* 1913.

Davis, Mary P. and Rock, Michael J. *Huning's Highland Addition Neighborhood Walking Tour and Armchair Guide,* revised by Ann and Jim Carson, 1996.

Dinnerstein, Leonard and Reimers, David M. *Ethnic Americans,* 1999.

Jones, Maldwyn A. *.Destination America,* 1976.

Kousoulas, D. George. *Modern Greece, Profile of a Nation,* 1974.

Kousoulas, D. George and Laliotou, Ioanna., *Transatlantic Subjects,* 2004.

Lamar, H. R. *The Far Southwest, 1846–1912, a Territorial History,* 2000.

Moskos, Charles C. *Greek Americans,* 1980.

Papanikolas, Helen. *A Greek Odyssey in the American West,* 1997.

Patterson, James T. *America in the Twentieth Century,* 1983.

Peck, Gunther. *Reinventing Free Labor,* 2000.

Psomiades, Harry J. *The Greek American Community in Transition,* 1982.

Riskin, Marci L. *The Train Stops Here, New Mexico's Railway Legacy,* 2005.

Simmons, Marc. *Albuquerque,* 1982.

Saloutos, Theodore. *The Greeks in the United States,* 1964.

Sophocles, S. M. *A History of Greece,* 1961.

Spidle, Jake W. *Doctors of Medicine in New Mexico: A History of Health and Medical Practice, 1886–1986,* 1986.

Xenides, J. P. *The Greeks in America,* 1922.

HONOR'S THESIS

Finley, Rose-Marie "St. George Greek Orthodox Church, Albuquerque, New Mexico," 1983.

DISSERTATION

DeMark, Judith Boyce, "The Immigrant Experience in Albuquerque, 1880–1920," 1984.

APPENDIX

Albuquerque City Directories, 1880-1952

People with Greek sounding names appear not only in the State Census, but in the *Albuquerque City Directories*. Listed below, during the years 1880-1911, are names of people that may be Greek. Were they? We may never know.

The population of Albuquerque in 1880 was 2,135

1880 was the year the AT&SF Railway entered Albuquerque.
1880:
    E. and Mary Nichols
    Ysabella Nichols, daughter
    Harry Nichols, son
    Clara Nichols, daughter
    O. Nichols, other than a direct relationship (?)
1883:
    J. D. Anthony, brakeman for Atlantic and Pacific Railway
    D. Soikes, waiter for Fresco Restaurant

The population of Albuquerque in 1890 was 3,785

1890:
    City Directory was damaged
1892:
    Ed Alexander, brakeman
    George Sides, Train dispatcher, he was Greek
1897:
    J. Nicholas, AT&SF Railway
1899:
    John Nicklas, machinest, Southern Pacific Shops

The population of Albuquerque in 1900 was 6,326

1900:
    John Nicholas

1901:
>   Mrs. G. W. Nicklas, housekeeper
>   Mrs. Lula Nichlas, laundress

1902:
>   The Alvarado Hotel opened

1907:
>   J. Nicholas, American Lumber Company

The population of Albuquerque in 1910 was 13,000

1910:
>   The Albuquerque, Presbyterian and the St. Joseph Sanatoriums all opened. The Santa Fe Railroad Hospital opened also.

1911:
>   Alexander Dim Kassimis, of Sidiorocastrou, Greece, worked for the Western Union Telegraph Company.

1913:
>   Frank Georges, Engineer for railroad, Greek
>   Frank Georges, Jr., Student

Below are the names and occupations of the Greeks found in the *Albuquerque City Directories*. Their businesses were all located in the very heart of downtown New Albuquerque. While scrolling through this list, notice how the restaurants changed hands and were owned by two or three Greeks at one time or run by a family.

1915:
>   George E. Thomas, later he appears in the 1930 Census as Greek, no occupation listed
>   Nicholas Goches ran the Fruit and Confectionery Co. on Central Avenue
>   Samual Vasil ran the Fruit and Confectionery Co. on Central Avenue
>   Nick Yanni was a shoemaker on Central Avenue
>   Peter Leakow (Leakan/Leakou) was a waiter for the Albuquerque Café
>   Arthur Pappe was a baker for Jaffa Grocery

1916:
>   James Pappas was a bootblack on Central Avenue
>   George M. Leakow was a waiter for the Albuquerque Café on Central Avenue
>   Peter M. Leakow was proprietor of the Albuquerque Café

1917:
>   Anthony Paulantos ran the Paul Psaltis & Co. which ran the Palms Hotel
>   Paul Psaltis was proprietor of the Mecca Café on Central Avenue and Paul Psaltis & Co.
>   Wm. Psaltis ran the Vendome Annex

George Carvos was a waiter for the City Café
John Goches was proprietor of the City Café
John Kallas was a shoeshiner on Central Avenue
George M. Leakow was a waiter for the Pullman Café
Peter M. Leakow was proprietor of the Pullman Café

1918:
Paul Psaltis appears to have been in the U.S. Army (WW I) and proprietor of Paul & Wm. Psaltis & Co.
Anthony Paulantos was proprietor of Mecca Café with L. Smith
Antonio Pappas was a waiter for the Mecca Café.

1919:
Theodore Pavlantos was manager for the Parisian Bakery and Ice Cream Parlor
Anthony Pavlantos, secretary/treasurer for Southwestern Lunch Company and proprietor of the Liberty Café
Daniel Paulantos worked in the Elk Supply Department for the Santa Fe Railroad
Gus Mproscaris was a waiter for the Liberty Café
Kostantinos (Gus) Koulas was proprietor of the Shoe Shining Parlor on Central Avenue
Sophia Koulas, wife
James Kliros was proprietor of the Union Shoe Shining and Hat Cleaning on Central
Louis Kliros came for his health, buried at Fairview Cemetery, TB
Paul Yannoui was an auto mechanic
Nick Goches was a patient in the Albuquerque TB Sanatorium
John Miskiostis was proprietor of the City Café

The population in Albuquerque in 1920 was about 30,000

1920:
Gust Bruskas was a waiter for the Mecca Café
Pelahia Bruskas, wife
Spiros Mpogdanos was proprietor of the New Mexico Candy Kitchen
Angeles Mazas was an ice cream maker for the New Mexico Candy Kitchen
George Bucus was a meat cutter for the Highland Meat Market
Lena Bucus, wife
Lena Bucus worked at an Inn
Alexander Janos proprietor of the De Luxe Café
Angela Janos, wife
Nicholaus Triandes proprietor of the De Luxe Café
John Kouteles was proprietor of the De Luxe Café
James Galanis was a waiter at the De Luxe Café

Nick Ganelfanos was a cook at the De Luxe Café
John Pappas was a waiter at the De Luxe Café, replaces Kouteles in 1921
Nick Parashos was a cook at the De Luxe Café
George Giannopoulos was proprietor of the Wholesale Candy Co. He brought his wife to a TB sanatorium where she died on June 3, 1925
Gus Koulas was proprietor of Joe's Shoe Shining Parlor
Tony Katsikas was a resident at the Alvarado Hotel (TB?)
John Liakou was proprietor of the Manhattan Café
Jim Sides was proprietor of the Manhattan Café
James Doules was a cook at the City Café
Phillip Ducas was proprietor of the City Café along with John Goches

1921:
Ernest Pavlantos was a helper at the Mecca Café
Tony Pappas was a waiter at the Liberty Café
Charles Poulos was a hatter for the Union Shoe Shining and Hat Cleaning Parlor
Gust Bruskas was proprietor of the Southwestern Lunch Co.
George Pappadakus was a waiter for the 5 and 10¢ Hot Lunches

1922:
Theodore Pavlantos was proprietor of the Mecca Café, Alpha Apts., and Liberty Café #1 on Central Avenue
Anthony Pavlantos was manager of the Southwest Lunch Co. and proprietor of the Liberty Café #2 on First St.
George E. Thomas was proprietor of the Liberty Café #2
Arthur Kaniamou was proprietor of the Liberty Café #2
Anthony B. Pappas was proprietor of the Albuquerque Candy Shop
Peter Bruskas was a bus boy for the Liberty Café
John Chaknos was proprietor of the 5 and 10¢ Hot Lunch
John Janos was proprietor of the 5 and 10¢ Hot Lunch
Peter Janos was proprietor of the 5 and 10¢ Hot Lunch
B. D. Karman was manager of the Delmonico Café
James P. Karman was a cook for the Delmonico Café

1923:
Bessie Pavlantos, wife of Anthony Pavlantos, first appears
Anthony Pappas was proprietor of the Thirty Seven Hundred Café
James Pappas was a cook for the Delmonico Café
Mike Pappas was a patient at the Jameson Sanatorium, buried at Fairview Cemetery
Gus Bruskas and Anthony Pavlantos were proprietors of the Liberty Café
George Christofides was proprietor of the Thirty Seven Hundred Café
George A. Thomas, A. Pavlantos and Arthur Kaniamou were proprietors of the Savoy Café
George Stonas was manager for the Hellenic Social Club, 108-1/2 N. 4th Street

Jim Chrisofis was clerk for the Hellenic Social Club or *kaffeneon*

1924:
    Hellenic Social Club no longer existed
    Patience N. Pavlantos, wife of Theodore Pavlantos first appears
    James Ipiotis was proprietor of the Angel Café
    Anastasia Ipiotis, wife
    Spiros Ipiotis was a waiter for the Angel Café
    James Karman was proprietor of the Angel Café
    Arthur Kaniamou was proprietor of the Angel Café
    William Koklas, no occupation listed
    George Christofides was proprietor of the Colonia Café
    Alexander Pappas, confectioner
    John Hantzes was proprietor of the Busy Bee Café
    Estella Hantzes, wife
    Charles Pouls was proprietor of the Union Hat Works

Charles Pouls.

    Cost Pouls was a cook for the Sunshine Café
    John Chaknos was proprietor of the Sunshine Café
    Mary Chaknos, wife
    Louis Poulos was proprietor of the Duke City Cleaners

1925:
    Arthur Kaniamou was proprietor of the Savoy Café
    Stratis Kaplanidis, no occupation listed
    Carrie Kaplanidis, wife

1926:
    George Poulos was proprietor of the Imperial Laundry
    Marie Poulos, wife
    Alexandra Carrigan, sister to Robert Katson and mother to Helen Morris
    William A. Pappas, no occupation listed

Hattie Pappas, wife
Gus Poulos was chef for the Court Café
Tony Tsimas was cook for the Mecca Café

1927:

Wm. Dolianites, no occupation listed
Charles F. Ellis proprietor of the Pig'n Calf BBQ
Nell Ellis, wife
Charles Ellis was a clerk for Plumkett's Grocer & Meat Mkt.
Hazel Ellis, wife
Gus Koulas was manager of Silva's Place

1928:

James Ipiotis, Steve Karman and Spiros Ipiotis left Albuquerque (the Angel Café), because business was very bad and they went to Santa Fe where they opened the Plaza Café. They went there because they had heard that business was better there because it was situated on Route 66.
Olga Pouls, wife of Charles Pouls, first appears
Nick Augustinos proprietor of the Sweet Shop
Regina Augustinos, wife
Hattie Pappas, Cozy Corner Confectionery
Peter Augustinos was clerk for the Sweet Shop
Angelo Glenn, no occupation listed
Arthur Marinos, no occupation listed
Rose Marinos, wife
James Spiros, Collector
Frank Poulos, no occupation listed
Constance Poulos
Louis Poulos was a clerk for the Blue Front Café
James Johnson was proprietor of the Blue Front Café
W. G. Mearns, no occupation listed

1929:

Nicolas E. Couloumbis was proprietor of the Sugar Bowl
Orlea Couloumbis, wife (Nora?)
Thos. (Lone) Karavaokyre was a cook for the Savoy Café
Daniel O. Askos was a barber and proprietor of Bennie's Barber Shop. Askos, was an accomplished violinist and played for the Albuquerque Symphony Orchestra when it was first organized.
John Coutsogeorge, 5 and 10¢ Hot Lunch
Gust Moutos was proprietor of the Coney Island Café
Evangelia Moutos, wife
John Moutos was a cook for the New Mexico Candy Kitchen
John Mastouris was a clerk for the New Mexico Candy Kitchen
George (Matsoukas) May was proprietor for the New Mexico Candy Kitchen
James Kamilas, was proprietor of the California Fruit Co.

The population for Albuquerque in 1930 was 45,430

Bill Chaco was proprietor of the Coney Island Café
Spiros Ipiotis was proprietor of the Coney Island Café
John Chaknos was proprietor or the 5 and 10¢ Lunch
Charles Ellis was proprietor of the Pig'n Calf Barbecue
Charles Ellis was proprietor of the Pig Stand Café
Alex Pappas was proprietor of Pappas Alex Lunches
Steve Dikitolia worked for the Factory and Mill Wood Co., then manager of liquor department
Helen Dikitolia, wife
Daniel Lewis was a cook for the Liberty Café
J. L. Mays was a traveling salesman
George Scolidi was a waiter for the Liberty Café
George E. Thomas was a steward for the Liberty Café
William Janetakos, no occupation listed
William Kirikos was proprietor of the Coney Island Café
Gus (Costa) Kakis was a cook for the K. C. Waffle House
John S. Cavalaris was proprietor of the K. C. Waffle House
James S. Cavalaris was proprietor of the K. C. Waffle House
Theodore Pavlantos was proprietor of the Mecca Café
Patience Pavlantos, wife
Anthony G. Pavlantos was proprietor of the Liberty Café
Bessie Pavlantos, wife
Gus D. Bruskas was proprietor of the Liberty Café
Pelagia Bruskas, wife
James Bruskas was bus boy for the Liberty Café than proprietor of night club
Peter Bruskas was night manager of the Liberty Café and then a night club
P. P. Satis was proprietor of the Savoy Café
Wm. Saltis (Psaltis?) was proprietor of the Savoy Café
Chistine Psaltis, wife
W. G. Mearnes was proprietor of the Savoy Coffee Shop
George J. Fellis was a driver for Robert Porter and Sons
Josephine, wife
Peter J. Fellis was a sales man for Coca Cola Bottling Co.
Rachel Fellis, wife
James (Jim) Johnson was proprietor of the Sunshine Café
George May was proprietor of the New Mexico Candy Kitchen then a cocktail lounge
Thomas (Matsoukas) Mays was proprietor of the New Mexico Candy Kitchen
Maria Mays, wife

Nick Augustinos was proprietor of the Sweet Shop
Virginia Augustinos, wife
Alexandria Carrigan worked as a domestic
Helen Carrigan, daughter (Helen Morris) was a cashier at the Court Café
John Soter, no occupation listed
Bessie Soter, wife Sales lady for Retail Department Store
Arthur Marinos was proprietor of the Silk Spotter Dry Cleaning
Rose Marinos, wife
Charles DeBerry, no occupation listed
Irene DeBerry, wife
James Morris manager of retail flower shop
Helen Morris, wife
Steve Dikitolia, no occupation was listed
Helen Dikitolia, wife
Louis Samaras was a waiter in a café
Stella Samaras, wife

The population in Albuquerque in 1940 was 59,424

George Addis was proprietor of the Laddie and Lassie Shop
Maggie Addis, wife
AHEPA Silver District Sanatorium
S. C. Alexopoulos, Superintendent of the Sanatorium
Tom Angele was proprietor of the BBQ Restaurants
Panayotis Arvanitakis was proprietor of the Town House
Daniel Askos was proprietor of the Dan & Steve's Barber Shop
Gladys Askos, wife
William Assimakis was co-manager. for the Liberty Café
Fannie Assimakis, wife
George Athens was proprietor of the Chili Bowl Café
Nick Augustinos was proprietor of the Sweet Shop
Regina Augustinos, wife
Peter Augustinos, was driver for a company
Lessie M. Augustinos, wife
John Benakis was a salesman for Oestreich-Haggard Agency Real Estate
Samuel Bezos was manager of the Court Café, came to ABQ. in 1945–1946
Frances Bezos, wife
G. D. Bruskas was manager of the Liberty Café, Anderker Cocktail Lounge and Yale Realty Company
Elizabeth Bruskas, wife
James Bruskas was proprietor of the Hi Hat Nite Club
Peter Bruskas was proprietor of the Hi Hat Nite Club and the U & I Café

Lorene Bruskas, wife
Jim Bruskas was proprietor of the Hi Hat Nite Club
Lorene Bruskas, wife
John Calamari was clerk at the Metropolitan Grocery & Market.
Gust Capels, no occupation listed
Fannie Capels, wife
JohnCapels was cook at the Liberty Café and Andeker Cocktail Lounge
Jane Capels, wife
William Capels was night mgr. for the Liberty Café and Andeker Cocktail Lounge
John Carlls was proprietor of the Carlls Cocktail Lounge and Pantheon Restaurant
Georgia Carlls, wife
John Chaknos was proprietor of John's Café
Helen Chaknos, wife
Georgia Chalamidas, widow
Louis Chalamidas, son
George Chalamidas, son
Roy Chalamidas, son
Peter Chalamidas, son
Tony Chamas was proprietor of the Chili Bowl Café
John Chirigos was sales man for the Coca Cola Bottling Co.
Helen Chirigos, wife
Gust Demas was a bartender
Effie Demas, wife

The population in Albuquerque in 1944 was 62,288

Gust Ellis was proprietor of the Blue Spruce Bar, Real Estate in 1944, came in 1943
Dorothy Ellis, wife
Gust J. Fellis, no occupation listed
Demetra Fellis, wife
John Constantine Forkos was proprietor of the P. K. Café
James Frangos was proprietor of the Canyon Café and Casa Blanca Bar
Bessie Frangos, wife
George Giann was a printer for the Gordon Printing and Rubber Co.
Elizabeth Giann, wife
William Janetakos was proprietor of the Vendome Hotel and Duke City Real Estate Co.
Niki Janetakos, wife
James Johnson no occupation was listed

Reba Johnson, wife
Costa Kakis was proprietor of the California Fruit and Grocery
Gus Kalevantas was a cook
Steve Kaplanidis no occupation was listed
Garofala Kaplanidis, wife
Paul Kapnison was proprietor of P-K Café and the Coney Island Café
Dorothy Kapnison, wife
Thos. Karavohyre was a waiter for the Imperial Café
Peter Karvelas proprietor of the Menaul Liquor Lounge and Ace Liquor Store
Angelica Karvelas, wife
Theo Karvelas was proprietor of the Menaul Liquor Lounge and Ace Liquor Store
John Katsikas was a cook for the Pig Stand Café
V. P. Katson was President of the Court Café and Curios; Katson's Drive-In, Blue Room Bar, Dutch Maid Pastry & Deli, and Hickory BBQ
Penelope Katson, wife
John Kazanas was proprietor of the Crest-Hi Restaurant
Nick Kessenides
William Kirikos was proprietor of the Pig Stand Café
Georgia Kirikos, wife
Steve Kirikos was helper at the Coney Island Café
Alex Koulakos was proprietor of Alex's Café
Gus Koulas was proprietor of the Union Hat Works and Shining Parlor
Sophia Koulas, wife
Jake P. Marhur proprietor of S & M Hat & Shine Parlor
Helen Marhur, wife
George May was proprietor of the Casanova Bar
Jamie Bell May, wife
George A. Mavromatis, no occupation listed
Fatima Mavromatis, wife
Angelo Mazas was proprietor of Grand Liquor Store
Josephine Mazas was proprietor of Mazas Fiesta Dress Shop
Bill Meares was proprietor of Doc's Barbershop
Sotrea Meares, wife
James Morris was proprietor of Morris Flower Shop and Carlls Cocktail Lounge
Helen (Carrigan) Morris, wife
Charles Moskos was proprietor of Nob Hill Shoe and Repairs
Rita Moskos, wife
George Nichols was proprietor of the Imperial Café and Big Chief Café
William Nichols had been a chef for the AHEPA Sanatorium
Anthony J. Pappas was proprietor of Serve Yourself Laundry
Angelina Pappas, wife

Rita and Charles Moskos. Photograph courtesy of Charles Moskos.

Gus Pappas was a salesman for New Mexico Leather Co. and bar manager. Blue Room Cocktail
Christine Pappas, wife
Harry Pappas was proprietor of the Cottage Grill
Tessi Pappas, wife
Nikita Pappas, no occupation listed
Voula Pappas, wife
Gus Patterson was proprietor of Gus Patterson Clothing Store
Rose Patterson, wife
James Pavlakos was proprietor of Crest-Hi Restaurants
Rose Pavlakos, wife
Sam Pavlakos was President of S & W Wholesale Outlet
Mable Pavlakos, wife
Anthony Pavlantos was manager of the Liberty Café
Bessie A. Pavlantos, wife
Fannie Pavlantos, daughter, worked for the U.S. Intl. Rev. Collections Office
Ted A. Pavlantos worked for the Duke City News as Circulation Mgr.
George Pavalantos no occupation was listed

Pavlantos family. Photograph courtesy of Mrs. Jenny Pavlantos.

Harry Pavlides, no occupation was listed
Europa Pavlides, wife
George Poulos was proprietor of Doc's Bar
Gus Pouls was proprietor of the London Hat Works and Shoe Repairing
Olga Pouls, wife
Alex Provas, no occupation listed
Florence Provas, wife
Paul Psaltis
Christina Psaltis, wife
Louis Samaras was proprietor of Imperial Café and Real Estate
Stella Samaras, wife
James Shinas was proprietor of the Pig Parlor Sandwich Shops
Andrew Tertipes was proprietor of Chili King Café
Ellen Tertipes, wife
Pete Tertipes was proprietor of Chili King Café
Dino Tufares was proprietor of the Cozy Café and Atlantis Café
Jeanette Tufares, wife
Jos. Vasilagias (Vasilakis) was proprietor of Imperial Café
Anthony Vasilakis was a clerk for ABQ. Publishing Co.

William Vlahakis, no occupation listed
Philip Vontirin was proprietor of the Canyon Bar
George Vrounas, no occupation listed
Stella Zavakos, widow

1948:
The Atomic Energy Commission negotiated a contract with Western Electric Company to operate the Sandia Laboratory as a private corporation.

The population for Albuquerque in 1950 was 145,673

The names listed below appear in the 1952 Consecration Album of St. George Church. The men's businesses or occupations are noted.

1952:
Constantine Alexopoulos, who in 1940 was the supervisor for the AHEPA Sanatorium, became partners with Gus Bruskas in the Yale Realty Company.
Panos Angelo was a chef for Tommy's Place
George Agrapides was a cook for Honey Dew Drive-In
Anthony (Sophia) Aleck was proprietor of the Central Pastry Shop and Café
Mike Argeanas was a sales man for Spitzer Elec.
Pete (Kay) Arvan was proprietor of the Royal Café
Dan (Glayds) Akos was proprietor of Dan's Barber Shop
Fannie (William) Assimakis was cashier at Coney Island Café
John (Pauline) Benakis was proprietor of the P-K Café and J and B Real Estate
Samuel (Frances) Bezos was proprietor of K & B Radio and Appliance Co., Inc.
Gus Bruskas was proprietor of the Yale Realty Co.
Elizabeth Bruskas, wife

Gus Bruskas. Gus Bruskas appears in The Historical Encyclopedia of New Mexico, Vol. II. published by the New Mexico Historical Association in 1945. Bruskas came to Albuquerque in 1918. He had taken a prominent part in local civic activities. He was state director for New Mexico of the National Restaurant Association and the first President of the Greek community.

James (Katherine) Bruskas was proprietor of the Hi-Hat Nite Club
Peter (Lorraine) Bruskas was proprietor of the Coney Island Café
Gus (Fannie) Capels
James Capels was a bartender for the Little Pump Bar
John Capels was a clerk for Hansen Cycle Co.
William Capels was a bartender
Ken (Helen) Carmichael worked as a realtor
John (Helen) Chaknos
George Chalamides was proprietor of the Liberty Barber Shop
Georgia Chalamides was a widow
Louis (Katherine) Chalamides was proprietor of the Town House Cocktail Lounge
Peter Chalamides was manager for the Town House Liquor Store
Roy (Lela) Chalamides was proprietor of the Town House Liquor Store
Thos. Chalamides was a mail depositor for the Bank of New Mexico
John (Helen) Chirigos was proprietor of the Little Pump Bar
John (Mary) Collaros was proprietor of the White Lodge Café
Steve (Irene) Collaros was proprietor of the White Lodge Café
Frank (Louise) Columbus was proprietor of the Pig Stand Café
Peter (Tula) Columbus was proprietor of the Pig Stand Café
Alex (Martha) Corondoni was proprietor of Al's Drive-In Café
Nick Couloumbis
Peter (LaJoy) Chumbris was a lawyer
Peter (Delia) Dallas was proprietor of La Fonda Bar
John (Stavrola) Dascalakis was proprietor the Canyon Café
George P. (Mary) Demas
Peter G. (Frances) Demas
Alex (Constance) Demopoulos was proprietor of the Unique Cleaners
Steve (Helen) Dikitolia
Kimon (Era) Economides was proprietor of the Grand Canyon Cocktail Lounge
Nick V. (Lulu) Eleamos was proprietor of the Shamrock Bar and Liquor Store
Gust (Dorothy) Ellis was proprietor of the Blue Spruce Cocktail Lounge
Mike (Katherine) Fabiani was proprietor of The Clock Café
Gus (Demitra) Fellis
George (Irene) Fellis was a sales man for Porter and Sons, Inc.
James (Bessie) Frangos
John Constantine Forkos was proprietor of the P-K Café
Angelo (Margaret) Gleen was proprietor of Hi Hat Nite Club with James Bruskas
Thos. N. George was proprietor of Tommy's Place
James (Camelle) Greches was a painter
Peter (Anna) Helis

Mike (Anna) Hontas was proprietor of Johnnie's Grill
Angelina Hontas (Daughter) was a waitress for Johnnie's Grill
James (Pat) Ipiotis
William (Niki) Janetakos was proprietor of the Duke City Real Estate Company
Gus Kakin was proprietor of the Balkan Grocery
Costa Kallimani was a carrier for the Post Office
George Kallas was a hatter for Atlas Hat Cleaners
Louis (Julia) Kanavos was a painter
Paul (Dorothy) Kapnison was proprietor of the P-K Café
John Kazanas was proprietor of the Crest-Hi Restaurant with Pavlakos
William (Georgia) Kirikos was proprietor of the Cactus Bar
Phillip J. (Gertrude) Kokens was proprietor of the Daytona Trailer Court
George (Sadiie) Kokolakis was proprietor of the Arrow Head Café
Alex Koulakos was proprietor of Alex's Café
Gus (Sophie) Koulas
Mike Kurgis was proprietor of Mike's Café
Peter (Helen) Laris was proprietor of Pete's Bar
Bill Laskar was proprietor of Laskar Photo Service
Anna Laskar was proprietor of Laskar Photo Service
Nick J. (Catherine) Louis was proprietor of the Bataan Drive-In
Arthur (Rose) Marinos was proprietor of Summer's Cleaners
Jake P. (Helen) Markur was coffee shop manager for Sandia Base
George (Jamie) May was proprietor of the New Mexico Candy Kitchen
Josephine (Angelo) Mazas was proprietor of the Mazas Fiesta Dress Shop
William (Sotrea) Meares was proprietor of Doc's Bar and Dispensery
Charles (Rita) Moskos was proprietor of Nob Hill Shoe Repairs
George (Mamie) Nichols was proprietor of Nu-Way Café
Ted (Edna) Niforas was bartender for Pete's Bar
Anthony Pappas was proprietor of the Golden West Cocktail Lounge
Angeline Pappas, wife

Angeline and Anthony Pappas.
Photograph courtesy of Elaine Pappas.

Gus (Christine) Pappas was proprietor of the Golden West Cocktail Lounge
Harry (Tessie) Pappas was proprietor of the Cottage Grill
George (Lillie) Pathos was proprietor of the Coney Island Café with Pete Bruskas
Gus (Rose) Patterson was proprietor of Gus Patterson's Clothing Store
Harry (Ruby) Pavlides
Miller H.(Mary) Pavlides was a Registered Public Accountant
Jim (Rose) Pavlakos was proprietor of the Crest-Hi Restaurant with Kazanas
Sam (Mable) Pavlakos was proprietor of S & W Wholesale Outlet
George (Jennie) Pavlantos was proprietor of the Liberty Café
Nick (Bobby) Petrakis
William G. (Helen) Petropoulos was proprietor of the Albuquerque Import Co.
Charles (Olga) Pouls
George (Goldie) Poulos was proprietor of Doc's Bar
Christ (Antonia) Psachos was proprietor of the Pig Stand Café
Michael Psachos was bartender for the Blue Room Cocktail Lounge
Paul (Chritina) Psaltis
Gust (Helen) Rakagis was proprietor of the Grand Canyon Cocktail Lounge
Betty Rakagis was a secretary
Lula Rakagis was a typist for Blue Cross Plan
George Rondos, Elm's Hotel and Apartments
Wm. (Athena) Roupas was proprietor of The Bowery
Louis (Stella) Samaras was in real estate
Sam (Theodora) Semos was proprietor of the New Kiva Café
John (Bessie) Soter
Mrs. Jewll Spiros was proprietor of Jewel's Beauty Salon
Peter (Maria) Stilios was a waiter
Paul (Leona) Symon (photo below) was proprietor of S & M Hat and Shine Parlor
Andrew (Ellea) Tertipes was proprietor of the Chili King Lunch
Pete Tertipes was proprietor of the Chili King Lunch
Them (Clio) Thalas
Athan Tufares was proprietor of the Depot Café
Deno (Jeanette) Tufares
Joseph Vasilakis
Bill Vlahakis
Louis Vrattos was proprietor of Louis Vrattos Jewelers
Bessie Vrattos, wife
Bill Zee was proprietor of a fixture company with restaurant supplies.

Louis and Bessie Vrattos. Photograph courtesy of Barbara (Vrattos) Vatoseow.

www.ingramcontent.com/pod-product-compliance
Lightning Source LLC
Chambersburg PA
CBHW022001100426
42738CB00042B/1100